BLUE JAY SLAYER

Published and Distributed by Aurore Press

Library of Congress Control Number : 2015933483

ISBN: 0692325859

~~First Edition~~ 978-0692325858

FIRST EDITION

www.aurorepress.com

Aurore
PRESS

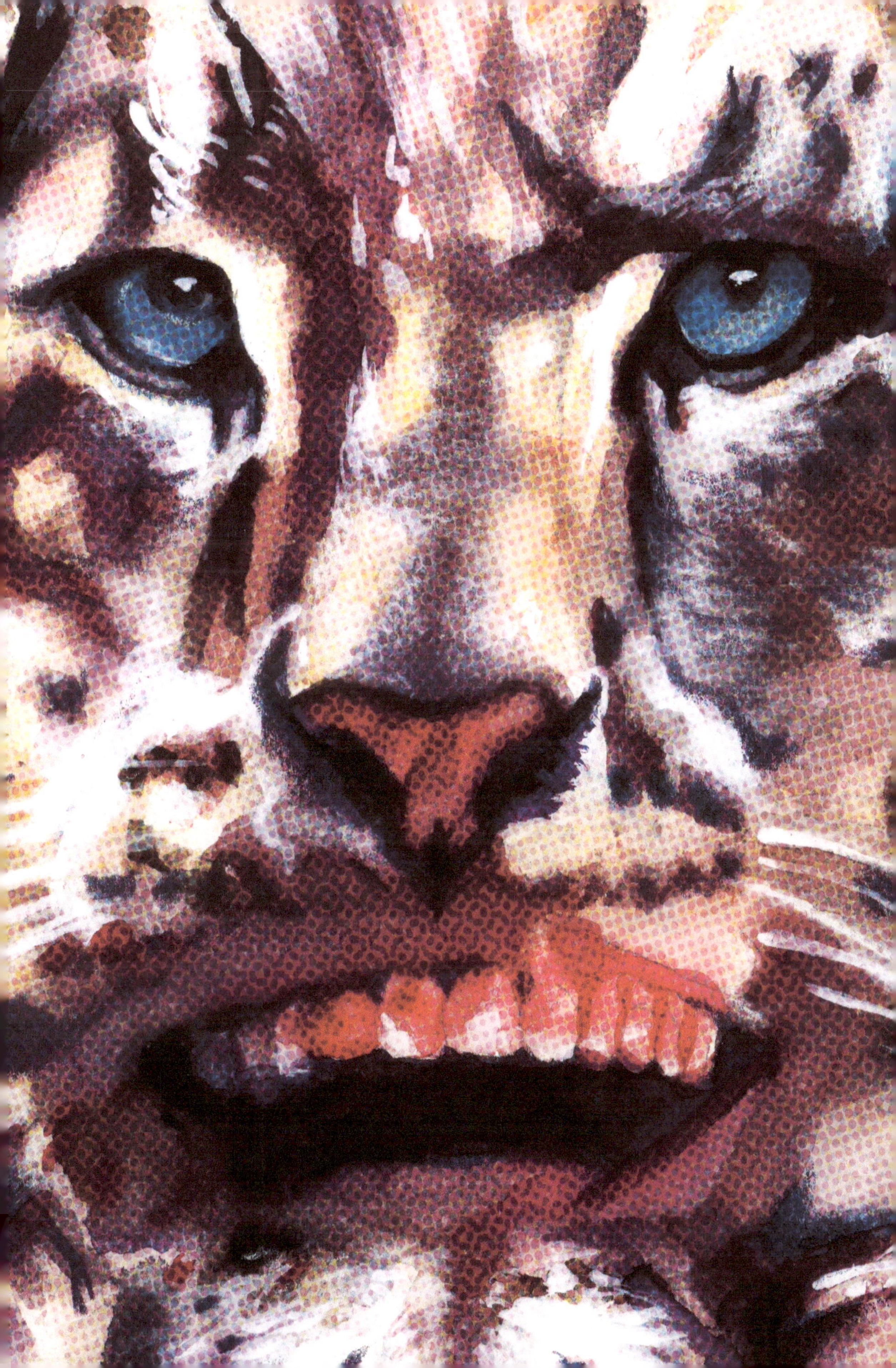

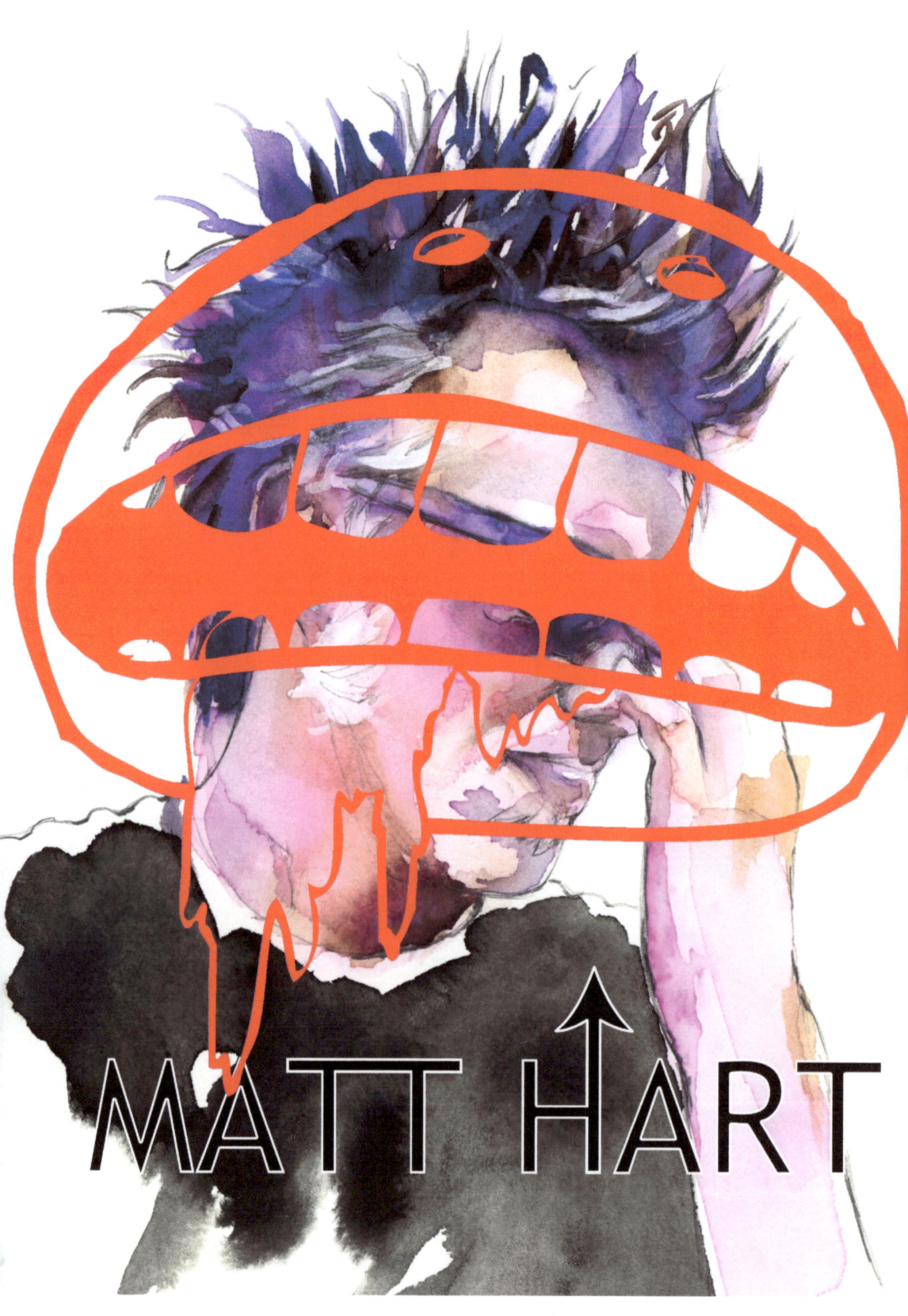
MATT HART

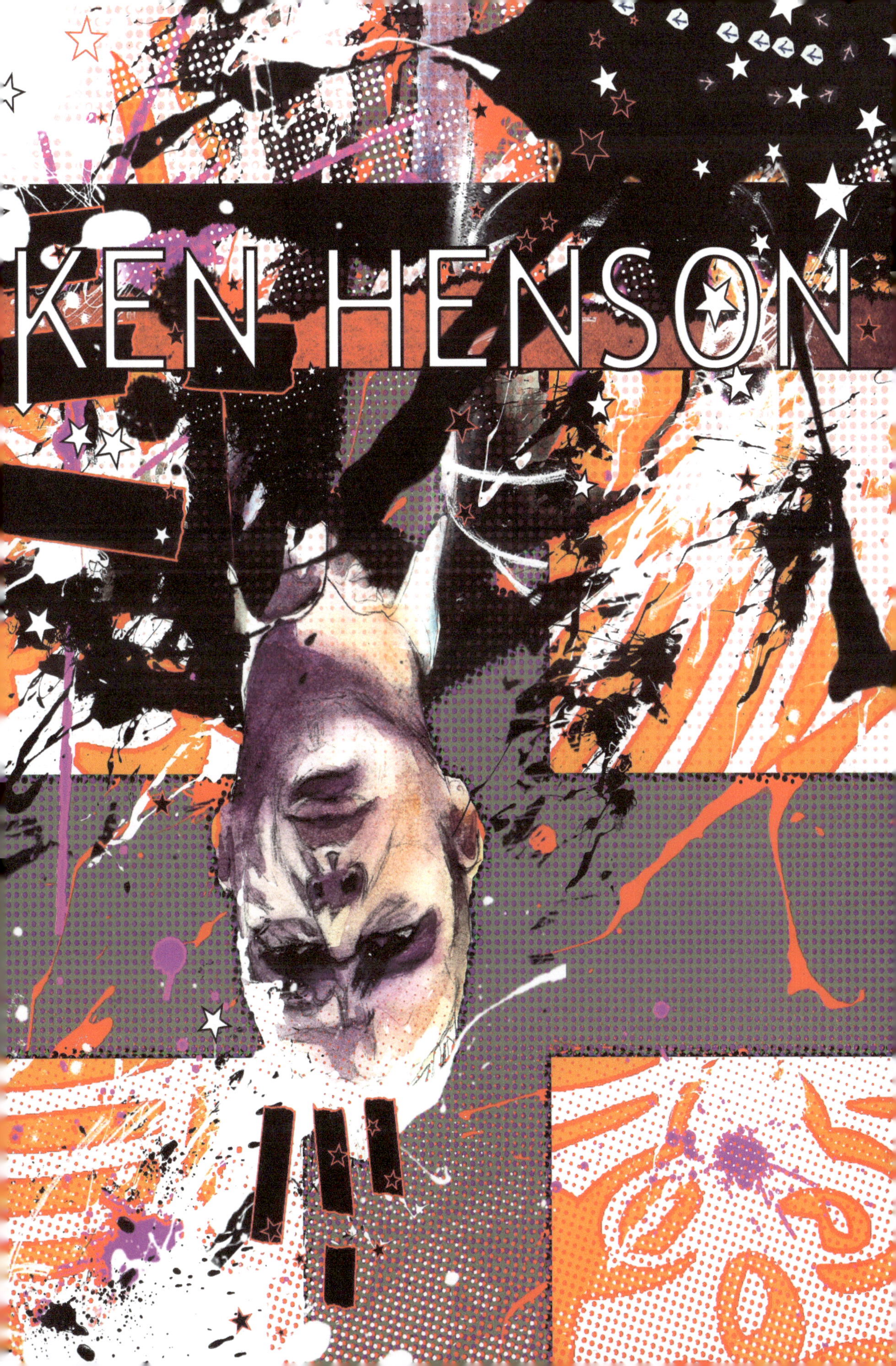
KEN HENSON

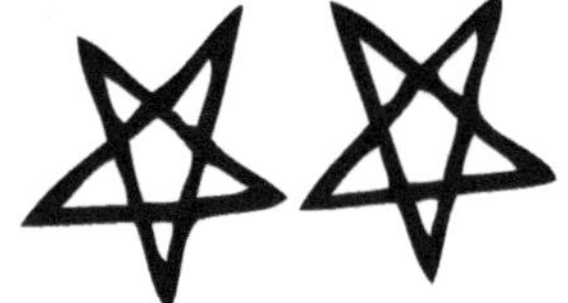

contents

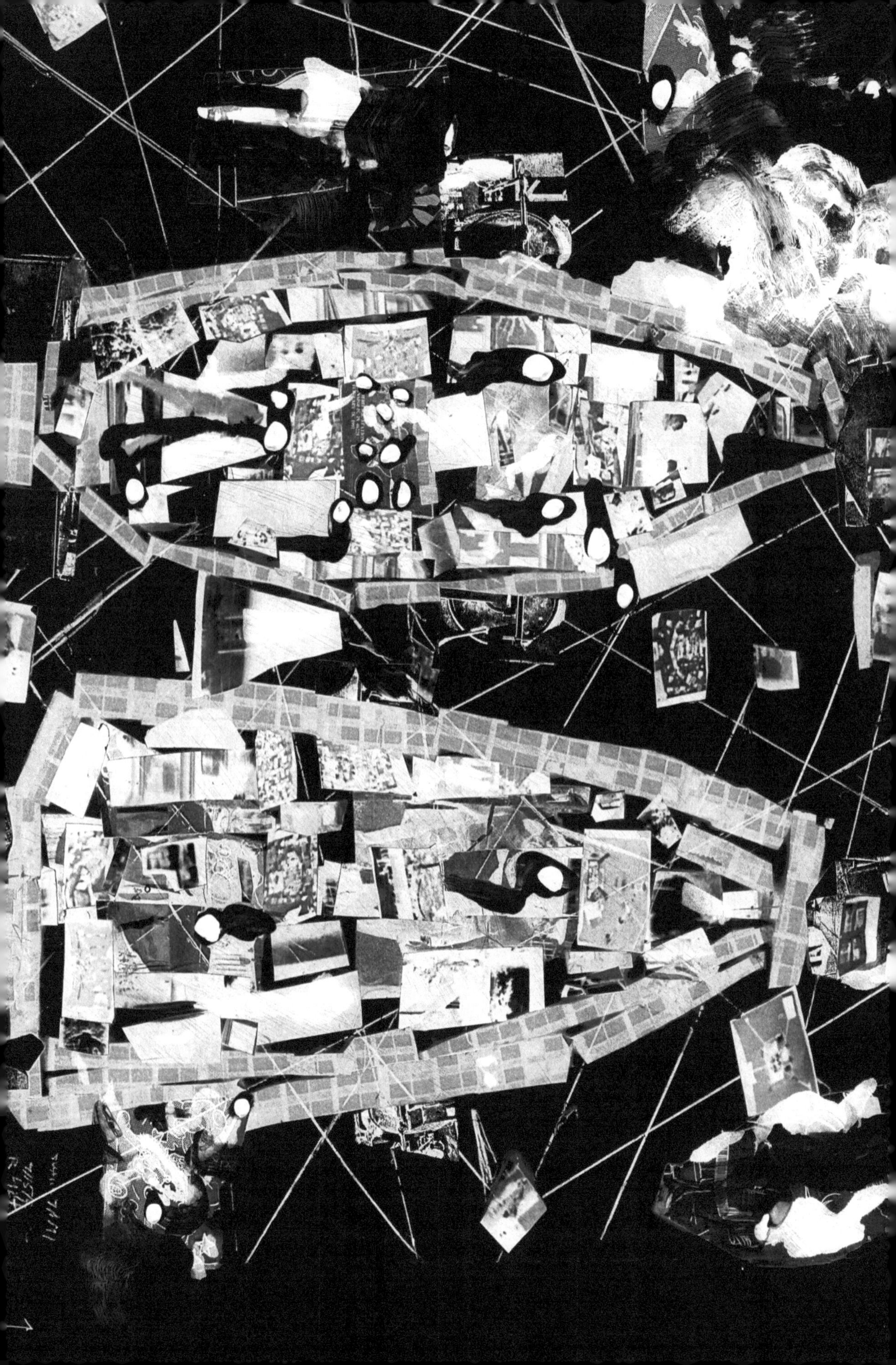

BLUE JAY SLAYER

→

BLUE JAY SLAYER

My wife awake or asleep.
My daughter asleep or on fire.
My brain in the weeds.
Alarmed or alarming.
Disarmed or in panic.
Is it not "doing better" for me to sleep

in the eaves? Is it "much worse"?
The earth so badly scorched
that nothing needs mowing, not even
my hair, which is glowing with black-

berries, a halo of knobby, dark energy.
The phone keeps ringing, but it's someone
Unknown. It's a guy with a grudge
in his pocket, a revolving door
under his tongue. He wants my family
to take shelter in an interior room
with no windows and stay there
until it's safe to appear again in public;
he will tell them when. My wife
and young daughter go missing

in the interim. I go
to the movies. In my bed
I'm watching football. In my dreams
the bloods win it. Then awful perfection
or a ratchety sound in the leafscape.

The air weeps its savings
and I go to the hole. I go
to the sharkery. The train clears
its throat, and I wonder
who's conducting? My daughter

hungover. My wife a spitting image.
In all the grainy news footage,
the Muslim protesters look bored,
or they look happy to be a riot,
since usually there is nothing else
to do in the village. Smoke billows out
of an Exxon or a mosque. I listen

to Slayer, but the blue jays in the tree
that I am walking toward are louder.
The grackles are louder.
I have been louder, but today

I am yearning. I tell the birds
I miss my family, and the blue sky
falls to its knees in mock grief--

little blue feathers from my pillow
in my teeth.

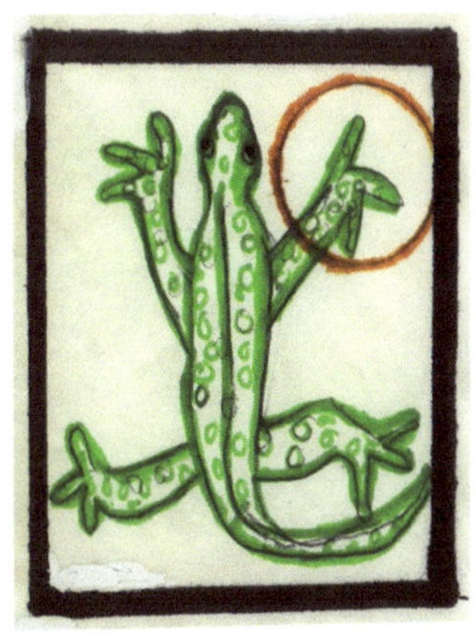

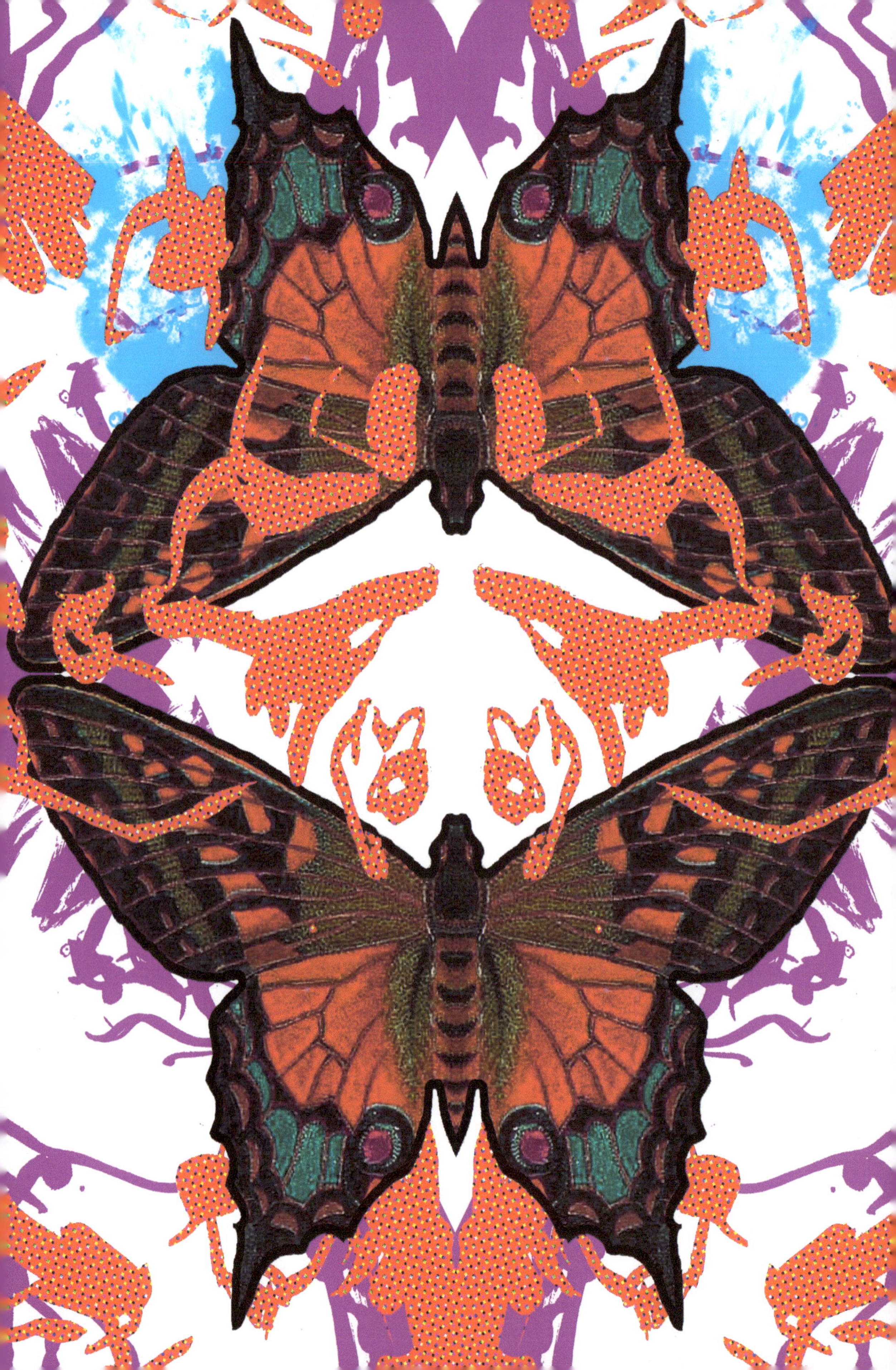

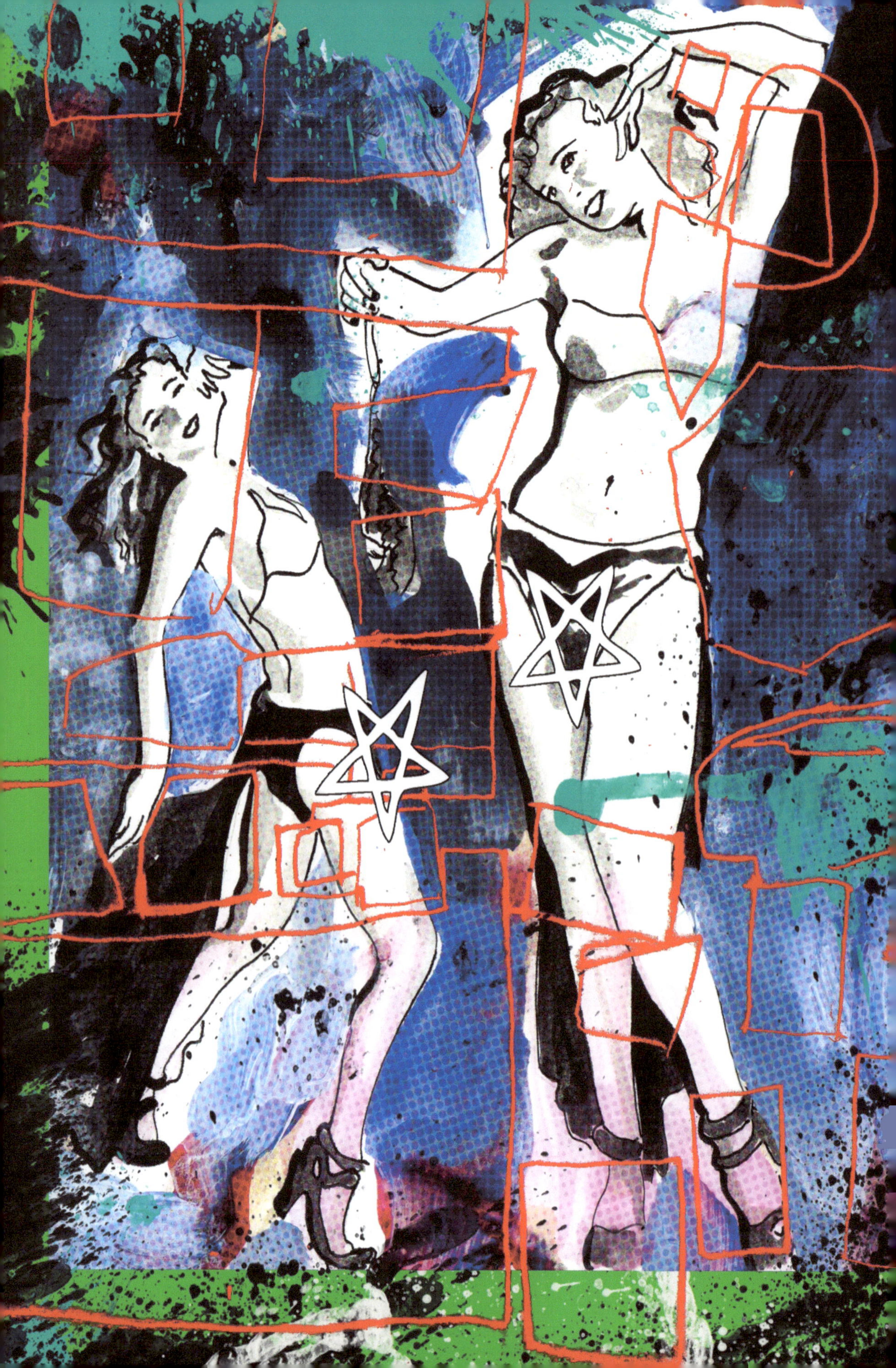

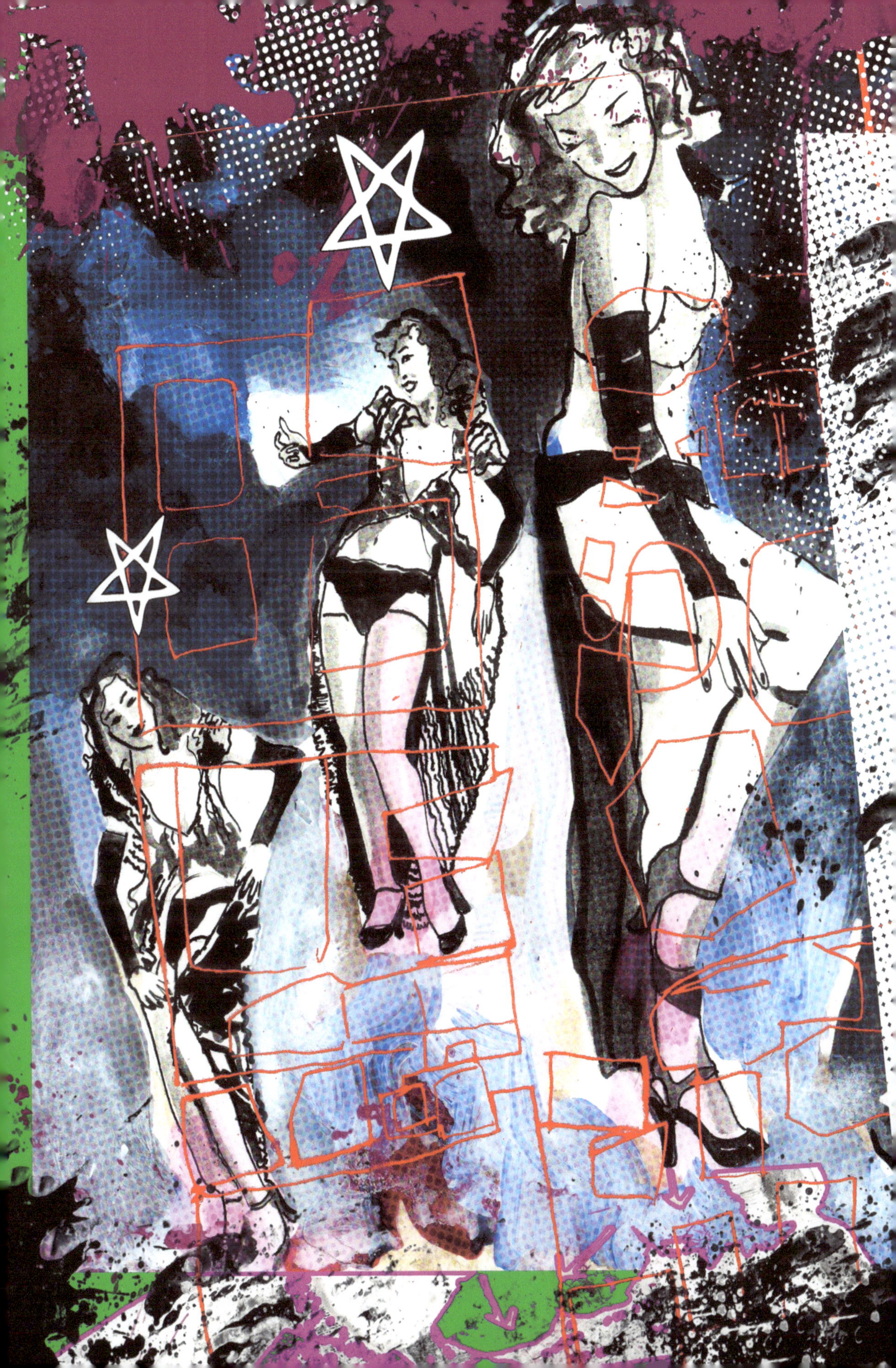

DUENDE

I go in the dark to the edge of the yard
or I go to the lake or the sea   The day-glo pink
soccer ball and the little girl await me there;
the old golden dog, she retrieves   All my dreams

say the same things over and over, say the hard
same things I already know and know
how to say, and which eventually will
break me and everybody to shards

of white paper or pieces of snow--inevitable
things I try not to think about consciously
The ambiguity   Sometimes, I sleep on my arms
accidentally, so wake up without them

'til the blood begins to flow   Only minutes ago
in my skull I was digging through a woodpile,
trying to fix a broken wildfire, or avoiding the lobster
by poking it with a stick   telling the Spanish poet

I've devoured his books   telling you, true love,
I am sorry for not saying anything sooner
about staying together, this nervous raw power
Never flinching from the presence of death

where we find it   We all find it   In the meantime,
I find myself nostalgic for so many things
which have never happened to me--birds' beaks falling
on my head causing rupture, the cries of people

places and things   Lists of flowers   Lists of pigs
I open my mouth, and a grizzly waltzes out
The leaves fall sweetly off the trees
of beer bottles

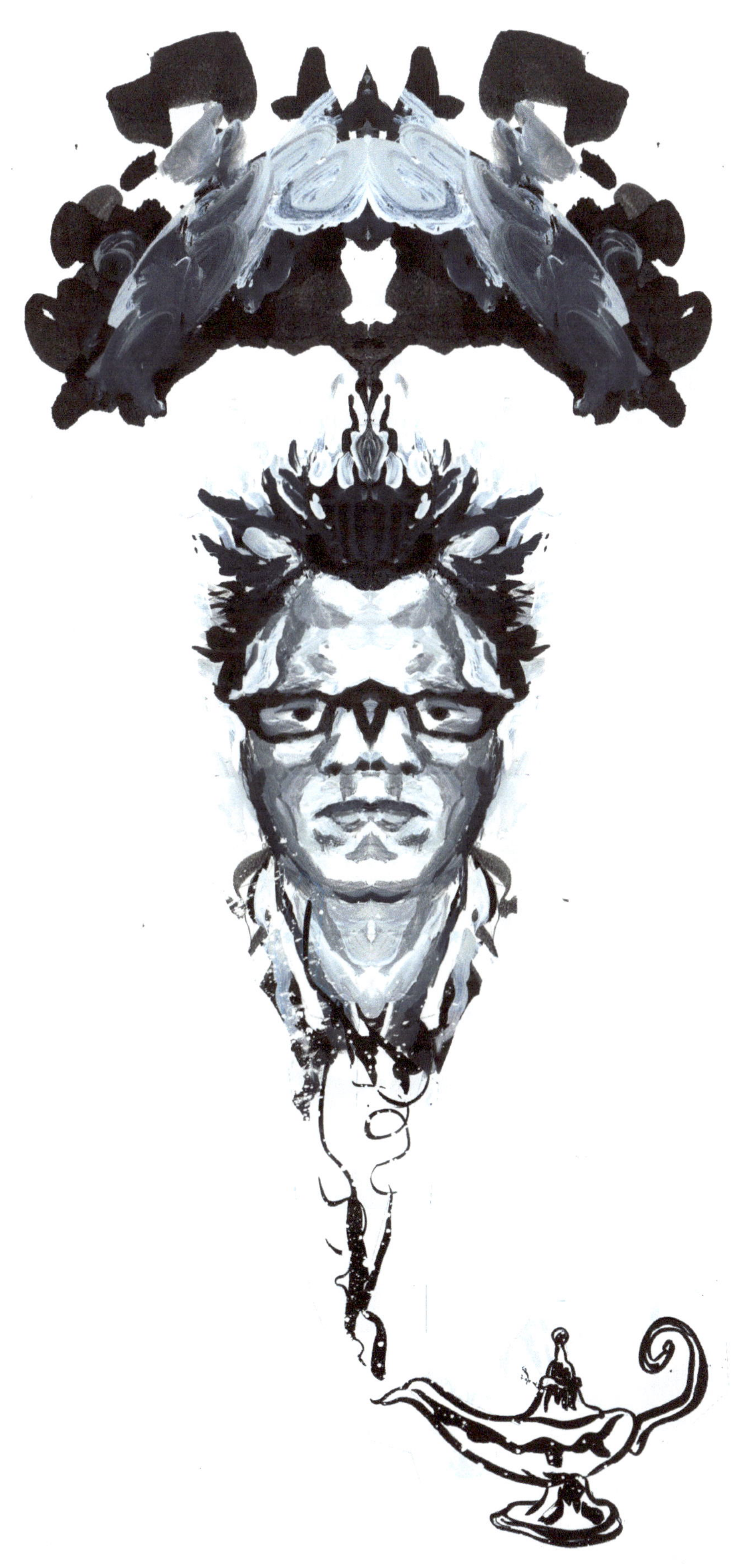

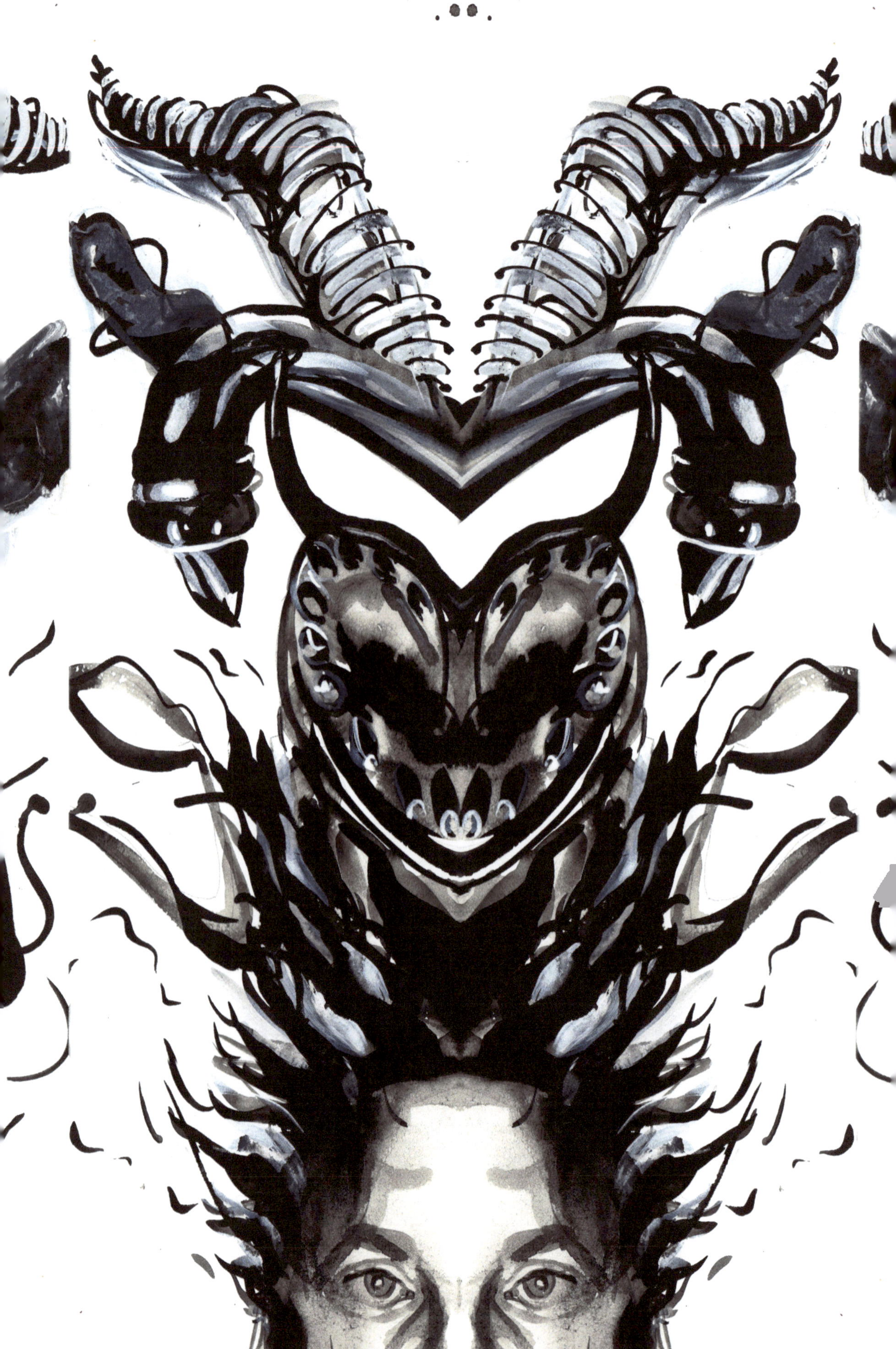

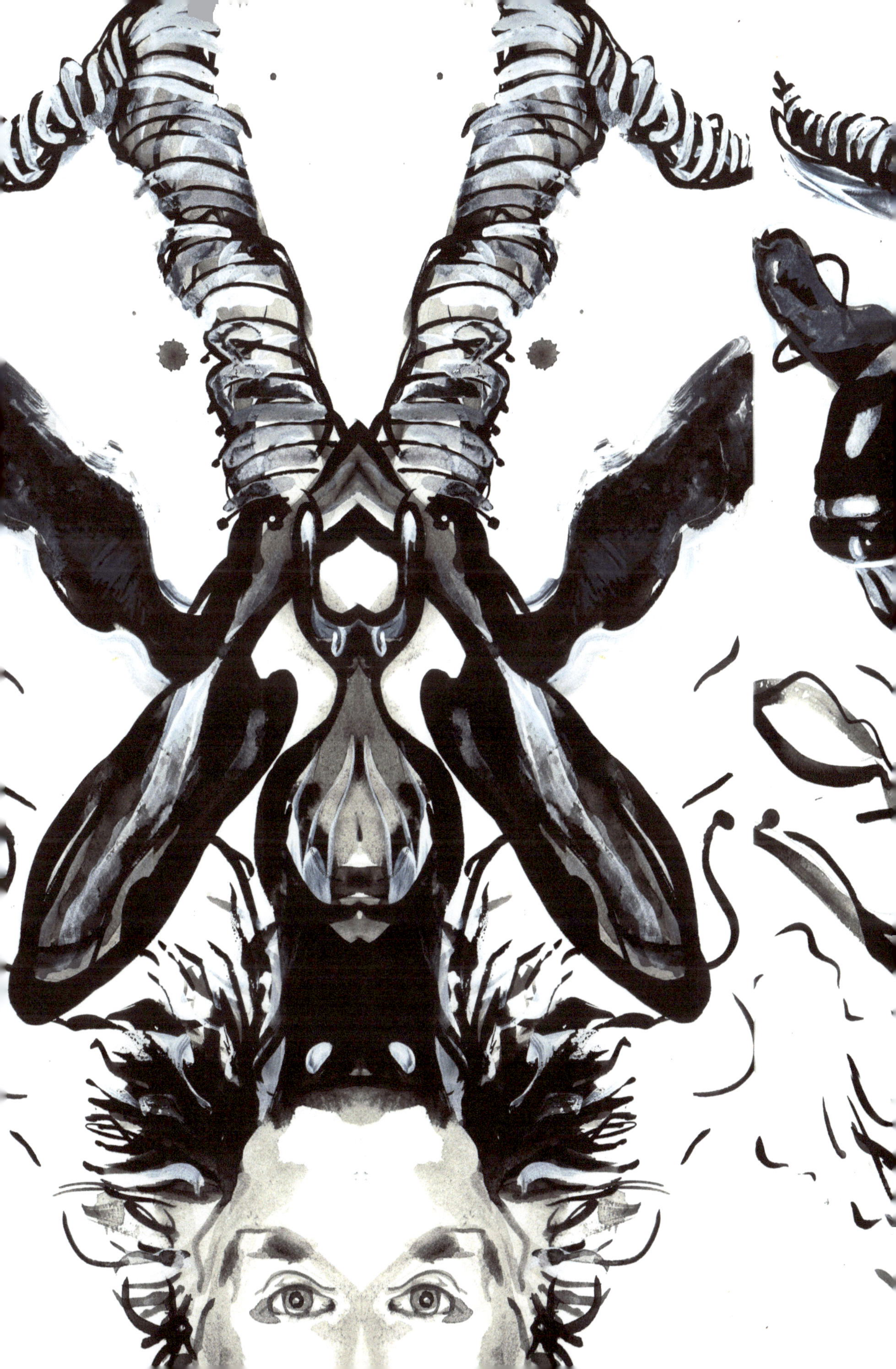

GRACKLE DEBACLE

Some minutes we study the bruise of an apple,
green as the sheep hidden deep in its meadow
My pants a murdered teepee with nodding
dark horses   The clouds clad only in axes

*

you call them ours, but I know them
as the neighbors'   The books on your desk
still refusing to squall   One of my hands on the small
of your backbrace, cold as the plums in the black-

*

metal icebox   I have no idea what we do
while it snows, so I shovel the pictures of thighs
wrapped in fat   My moneyed pockets   We roast
the large goat without thinking of summer

*

the lemon zest in salted waves of happy hunting
Bores we are called when we don't do the dishes
In the hills there is a monster, silos of grain
and a satellite antenna   He watches the game

*

while watching the game, pheasants and deer
all manner of protein   The three biggest
Vikings wander into a gymnasium, heads a little
out of it from all the heady damages   Danger

*

we embrace when the swords start to blow
the sticky words into a sentence   The lovely bodies
go to pieces when they see it in the offal   You are
wearing nothing, but a t-shirt with a rocket   Some flowers

*

blabber with tongues white as phosphor   You
shouldn't have vouched for the thief
with all your lights on   The raging of the dying
now completely horseradish   I take you to exile

*

in the rump of the piñata   When we arrive
the whole kitchen is spilling with domestics,
sacrificially speaking, and the ceremony
most finished, or almost   I am wooly

*

mammoth as the beach continues breaking
its promise   The curve of the landscape,
like a goddess or a shipwreck   I rush at the enemy,
and nothing is surprising, so I find you

*

in the arms we've been storing in preparation
for occasions like this one   I run the ghosts through
with a sharp paper airplane   So much intimacy
lost in the dogbowl   I thought I heard Vicodin,

*

but I guess it was victory, the lyrics overflowing
of your claw-footed deathery   Bathtub to rescue me
All the towles in the dryer with our under things   We make
blueprints that stand up to scrutiny   The scrutiny of detectives

*

on the scent of your trail, I squeeze your cheeks
from nose to tail when you sit on my lap and the beer pours
into us from sky and from ocean   We drink to the future,
so we aren't ever mentioned in history books   The best

*

things in chorus and multiplied by thousands   Now
we can live where the elevator takes us   The houses
fat as baby cows   The trees it seems lately
have been keeping us awake

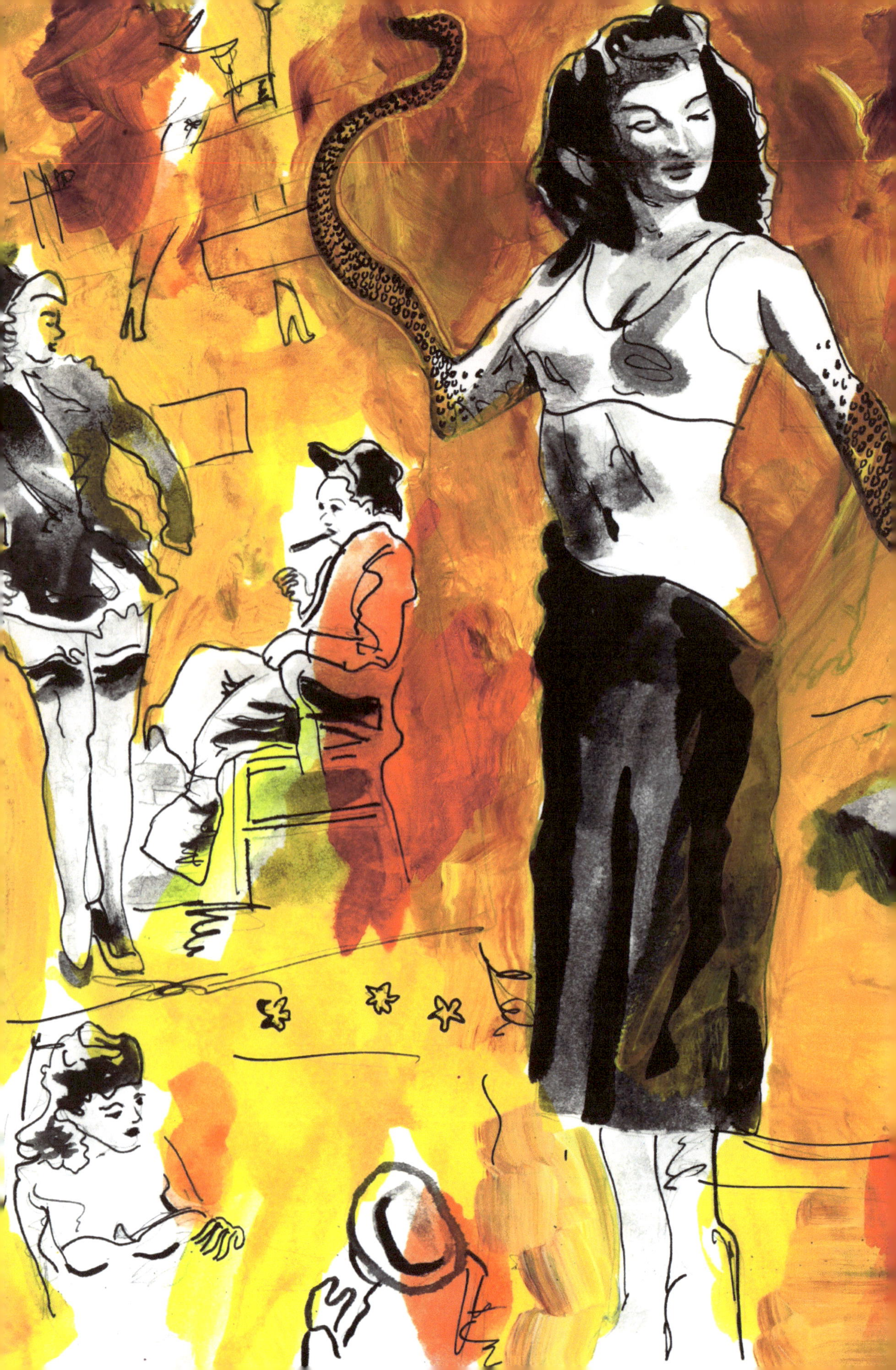

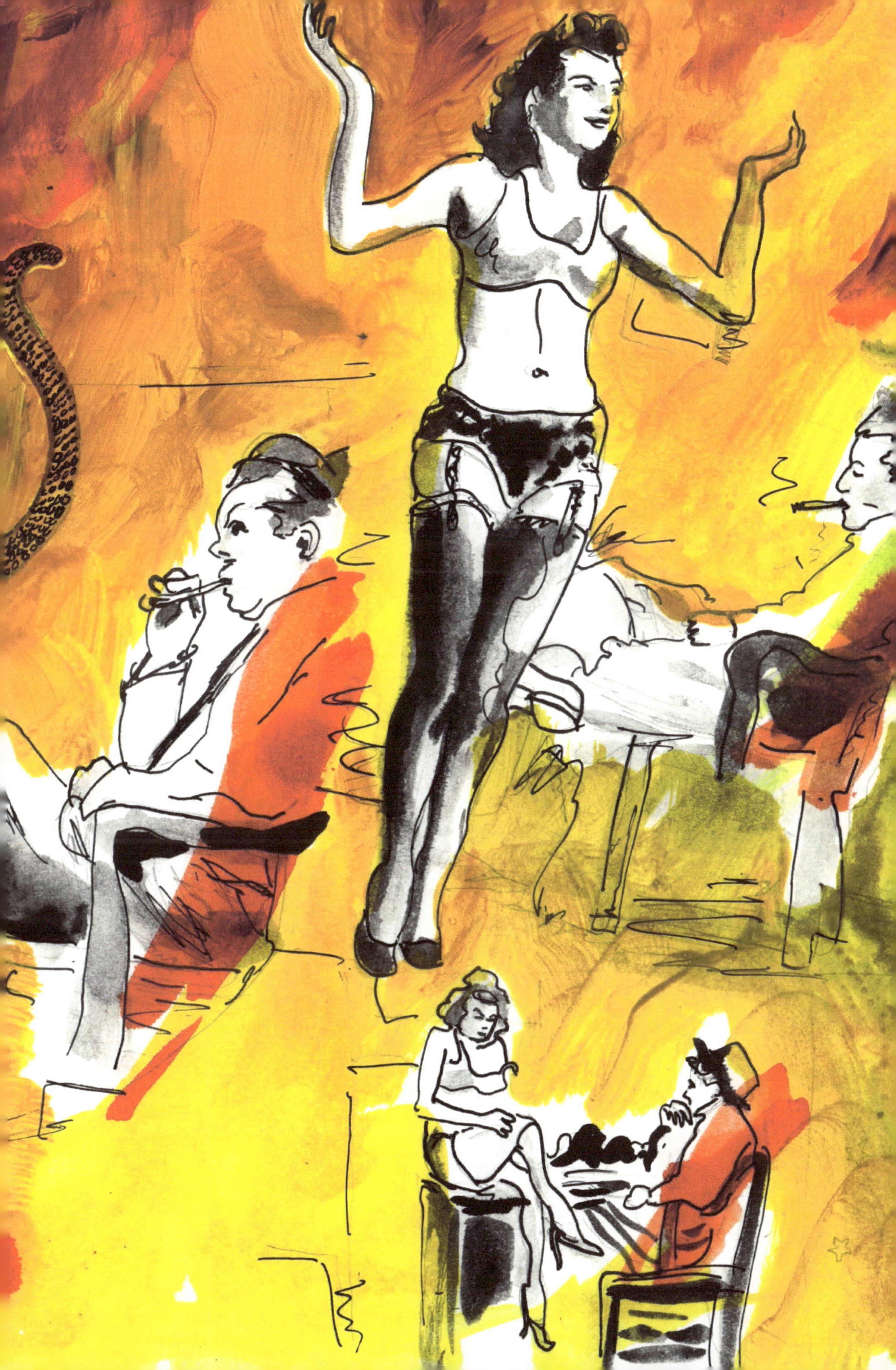

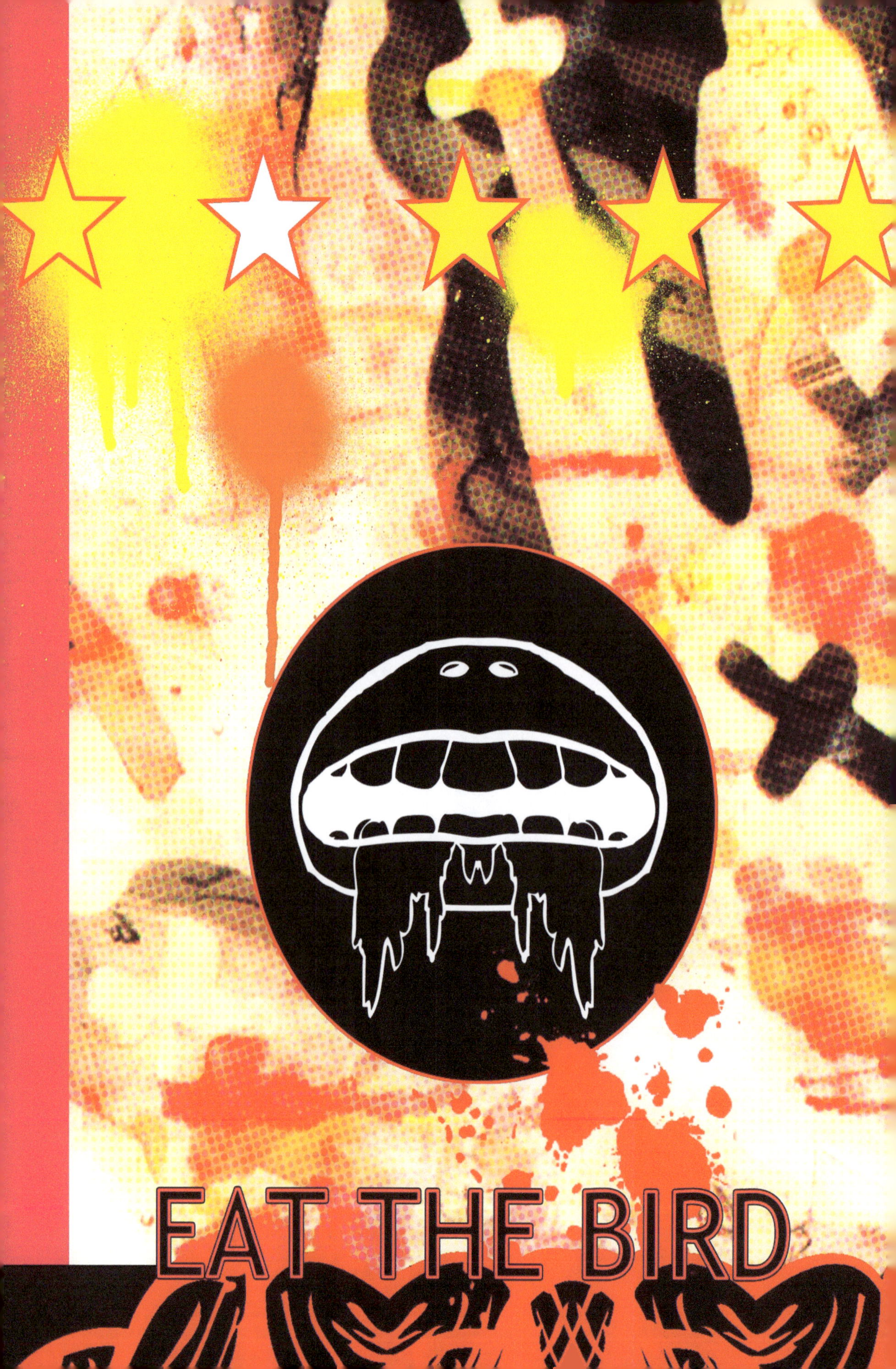
EAT THE BIRD

BLOWSNOWER/
WALKING DEAD

↓

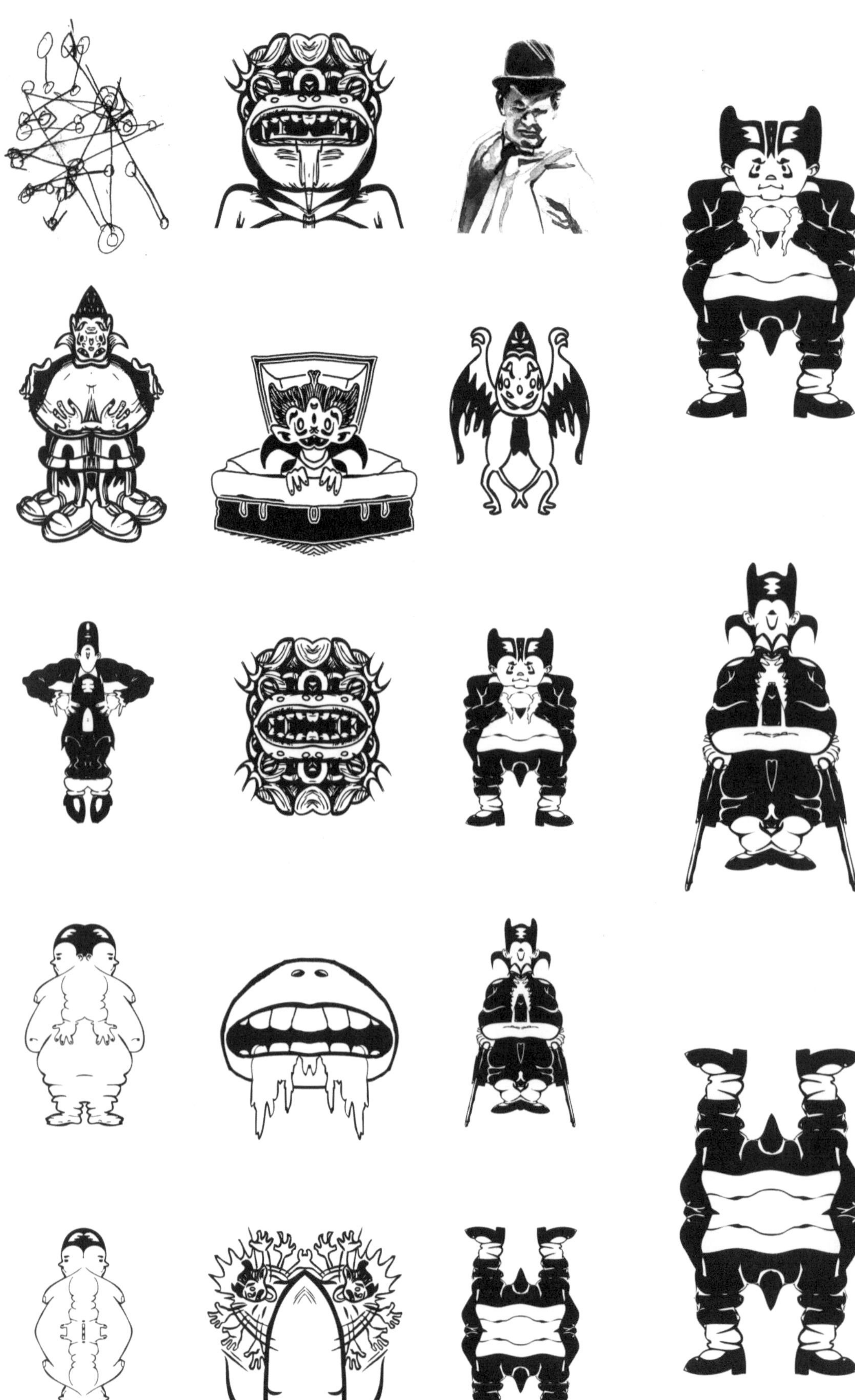

THE WALKING DEAD

is not a death sentence--
is not a sentence at all--
though it very well may be
the chorus to a popular song
or a description of the people
who let themselves sing along
with their arms coming off
and their jaws in the fields
for the hogs and the hawks.
It doesn't have to be a nerve-
end fraying. It doesn't
have to be the light dying
all afternoon. The mountains
keep swaying, and the noise
of the foghorn sounds more
like breathing than it does
like the dreams of clouds
to be more substantial
than butter. Even the sun
melts into the horizon
over and over and over,
then it rises. The ~~spirits~~
sourdough
rises. The spirits of owls
and squirrels wake up.
The walking dead wander
in a herd without stopping
is a sentence descriptive
of the settling frost, a box
of glazed doughnuts,
pot of coffee.

NOISEFLOWERMAKER

Trying to make sense
of the restlessness
of being, instead of being
with my family, instead of

driving into town eating
an orange or going running
to a movie   I bend down
to smell the noise-

flowers and hear nothing
but my own disturbance
A ribbon snake run over
in the street with a bicycle,

the ancient cat's cry before
we put her to sleep   I can't
tell the difference anymore
between Godzilla and a

wind-up nun breathing sparks
on the kitchen counter
at a kielbasa   Static is
everywhere   Restlessness

is in me   Hubbub
and thralldom   King
black hole   I am so
impatient folding laundry

I forget it
My soul wadded up
in the 21st century

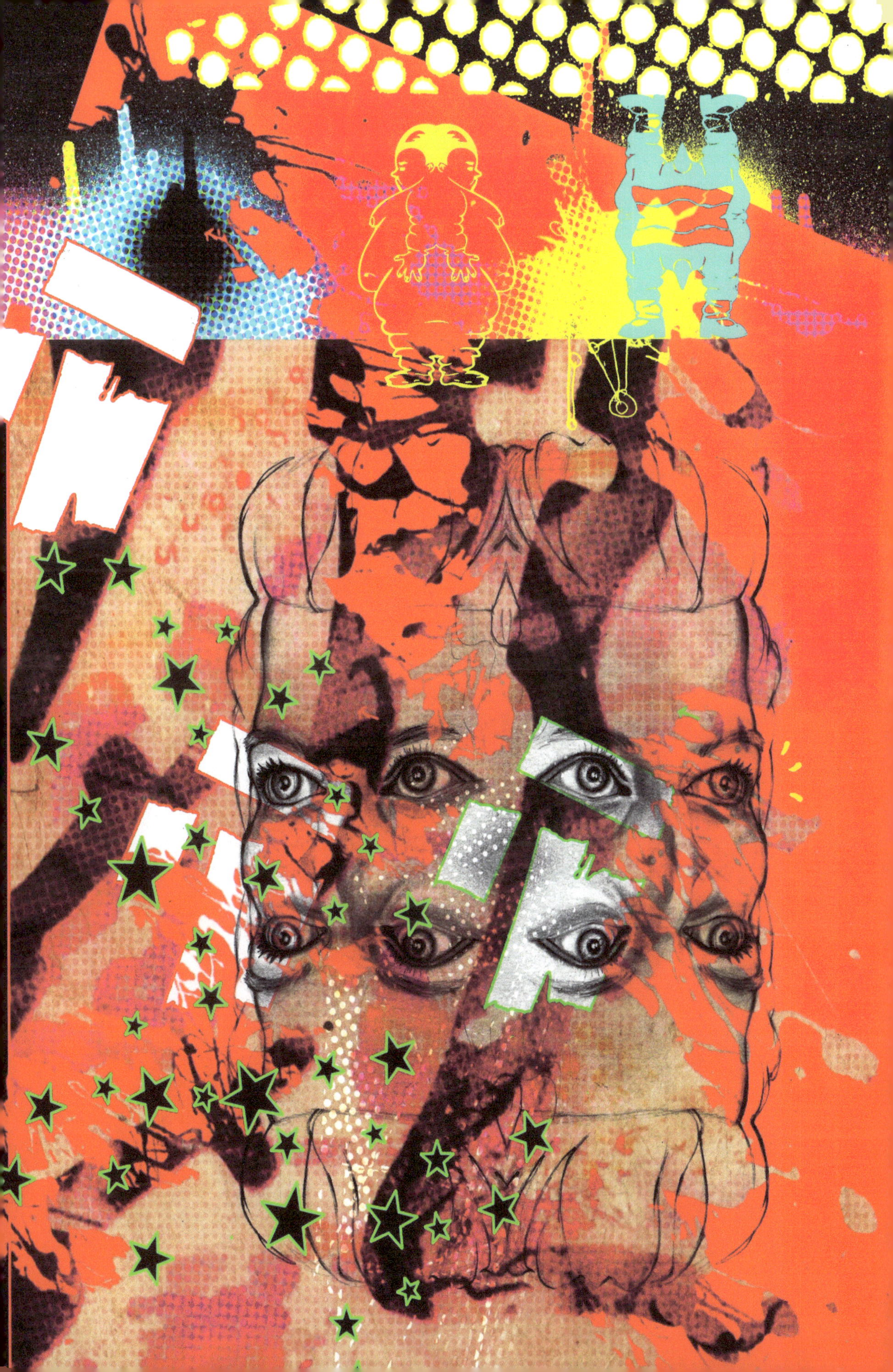

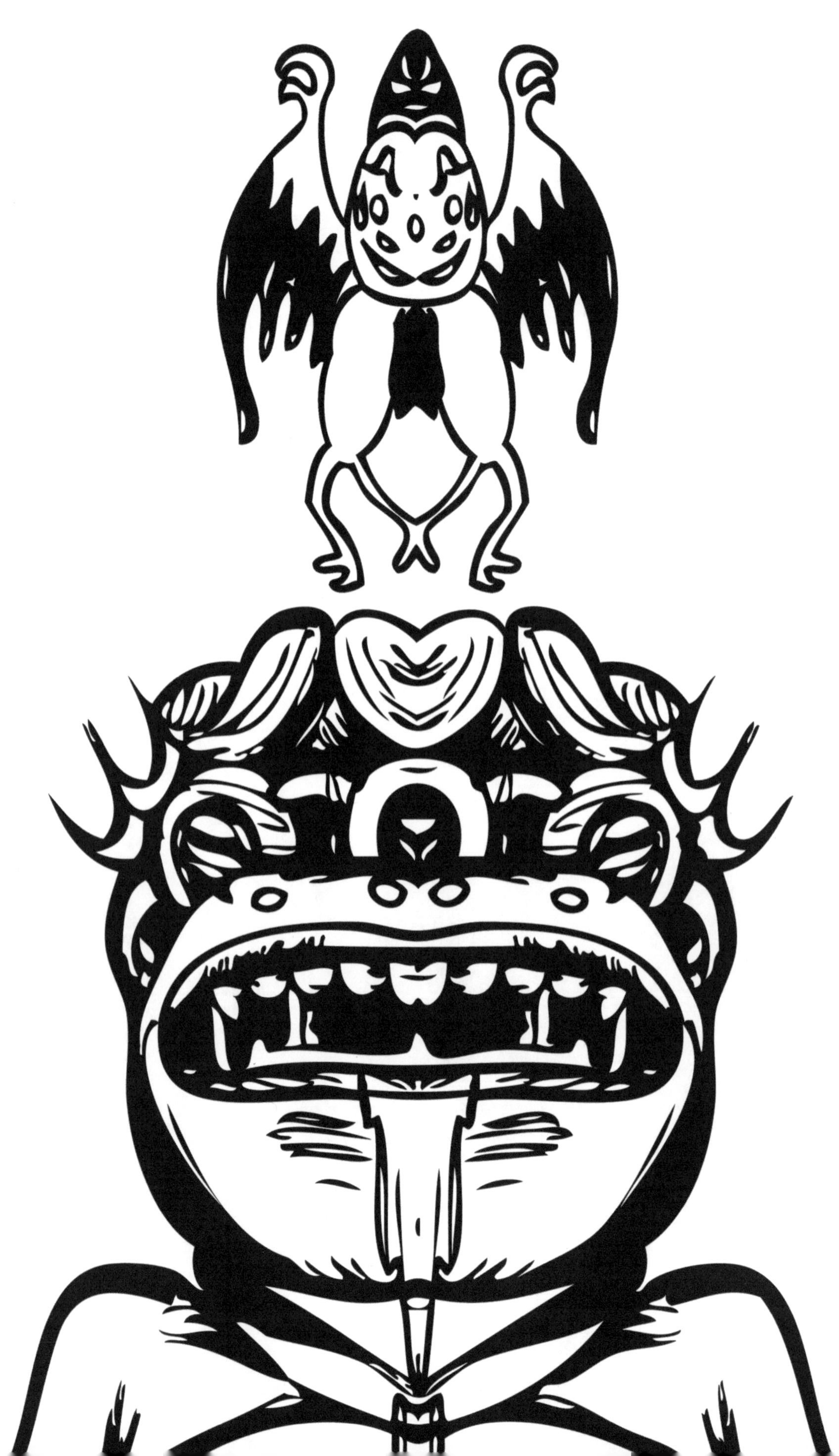

WITH GHOST ATTACHED

I wonder at those people who are
no more   They don't know
how awake I am

worrying my head into a garden hose
of doom, a wasp of last chances
and lemon ricotta, all of which sounds
a lot more ridiculous than I mean it   I mean it

while the memories of houses ~~flickerxthroughxme~~
I've lived in
flicker through me, like the juice of an orange
or an apple   I'm delirious with snoring, or

an illness nefarious, my calves cramping up
something wicked   No rest for the men and women
in the factory aglow   Light dusting of snow
And my neighbor with his dog

out walking at 5:30 in the morning
I'm drinking water in the moonlight
as it hurls itself through the living room

window without breaking   This life
I love will eat my bones   My mother doesn't know
and my father doesn't know   My wife asleep ~~upstairs~~
upstairs doesn't know   Even the owls   xxx

in their maniac trees   O nothing
machinery explaining

RABBIT'S FOOT

A rabbit's foot and a rabbit's ghost
don't often travel together
or in the same breath as part
of the same light or darkness,
but right now both are
in my pocket--one to give me
energy, the other to watch over me,
protect me from evil and clouds
on the march   I would like to win
the lottery, but I never play the lottery,
so really I would just like a lot of green
racket to fall from the sky and make me rich
and immortal, but if that's not possible
I'll settle for love, which is a higher value
anyway, and even in all its glory, also
marvelously disruptive, so more like coughing up
a geranium than like going out for a walk
and running into the moon, or realizing
that every single experience one ever has is
perfect and coated in a fine shimmery gloss,
which is not meant to diminish its beauty, but
to enhance its mysterious wash over us
A soft light leaps in the periphery

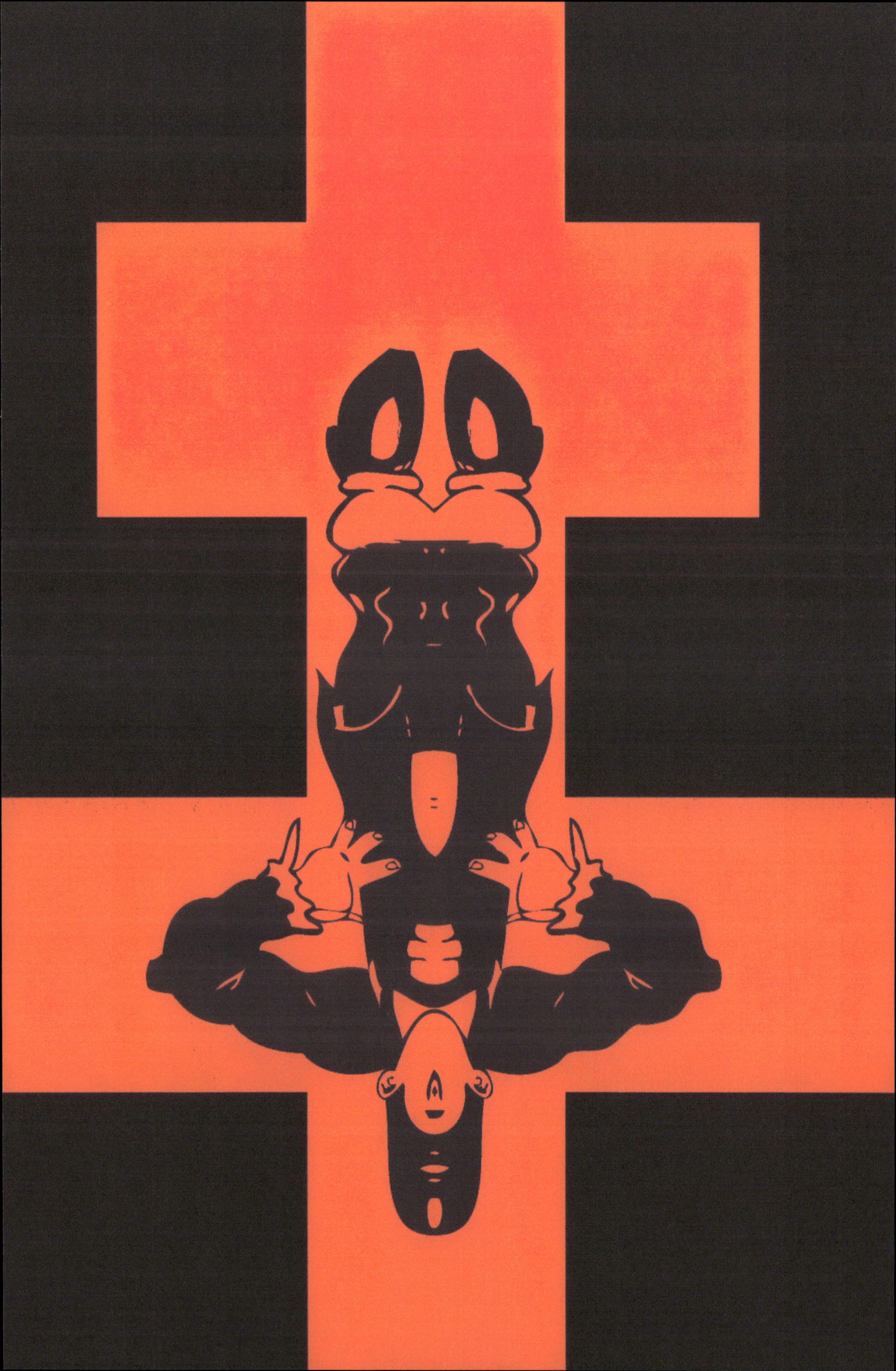

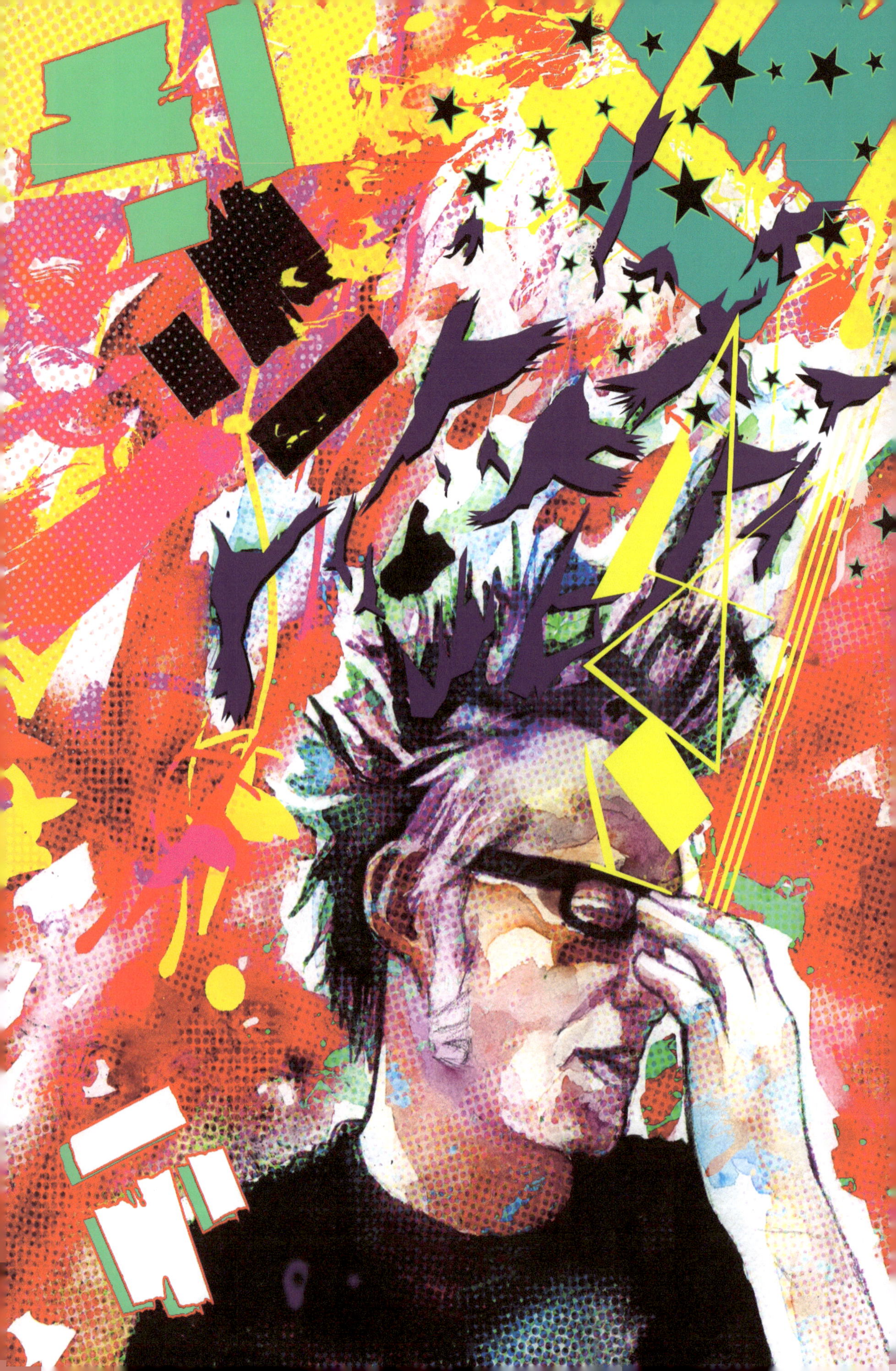

PEOPLE POUR PEOPLE

and a child bends down
to pick a wildflower   What kind
of wildflower to the child

is unknown   Buttercup
or bumble bee   The world
acrobatically lurches at me

The child says none of the above
The child says none of these
Mine eyes have seen the glory

in the alcoholic shrubbery,
blurry from the country and the fumes
and the city   It's true, I really can't see

the storm in your oak tree,
but stumble down the basement stairs
to see what something's dying there

The tone in atonement has a lot to do
with harmony   People pour people
in the streets like beer

GOLDEN

In this one, you start by climbing
out of your head, then go into the clearing
and run around in circles, not knowing

quite what to do next... You eat a hawk,
that's what you do next--snatch it--
right out of the air with your fork,

and the feathers drip down your face,
which is when you know you've got something
really special this time, so you chew and try

to fly, and it's as if the spirit of the airport--
of all the airports--is with you, hollow-
boned and full of blood. The helicopters

have always been a joke, but now suddenly
they aren't, green and blue and lined with gold.
You eat some and roll on your back

into a building. The building collapses
or it falls into a picnic. Whales come up
to the surface for your birthday and blow

some liquid paper through a hole ~~inxthexsnow~~
in the snow. That's when the sun
comes undone, and it's an opera. You

carve your bright initials on the trunk
of your penis. Or some dumbass
football player. Or Congress.

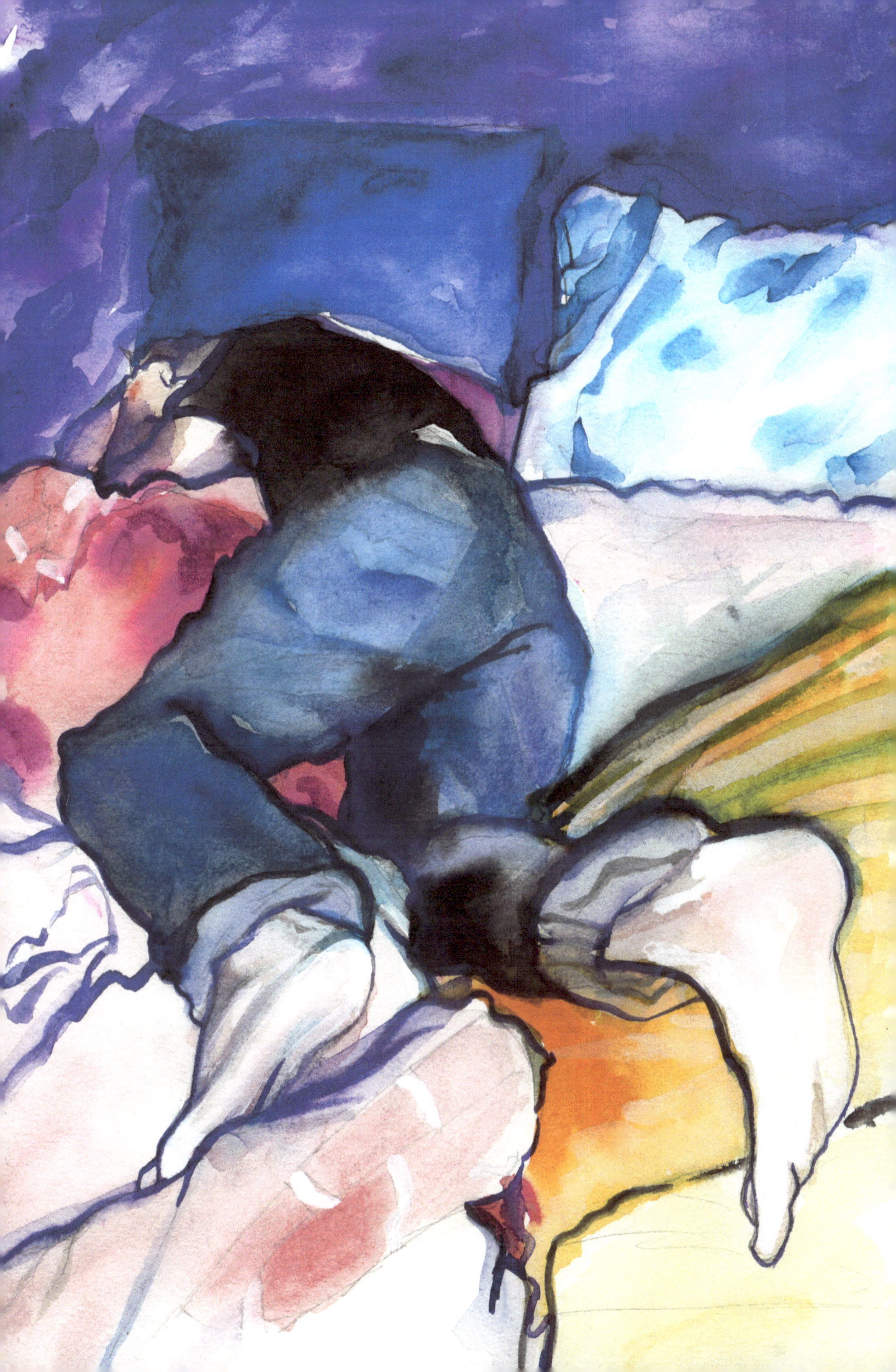

THE TV IS ON THE TV IS ON THE TV

is always on, which is a lie,
and it's Sunday, which is
the truth, and there's a face
in the corner blooming
with colorful language,
so I look at it for exactly
eleven seconds, trying
to imagine the most
honest way to tell you
an orange, but then
I realize that the most
honest way has nothing
to do with the imagination,
at which point I conclude
that honesty isn't the best
policy, but also that that
orange sure looks delicious,
and if we only had some
little fishes, some eggs
and a crusty piece of bread,
maybe a knife, we could eat
a still life for breakfast,
and right then and there
all the blazing-est art
would fly right out
the window, chirping
its hurt at the sunnier
dispositions, which is
another way of saying
even the bright things are
awfully bright, and
additionally, that face
in the corner is opening
its mouth, revealing
its satellites' gratuitous
violets, "Give me
my motherfucking
feelings," it reminds us
not to be an image
of an image of an image
nor to come any closer.
Mystery is crucial
for the good
of human being,
all running together

with the yolk of an egg
or the zest of an orange
and two or three
other things,
some crying,
some screaming,
all the stars
in one bite.

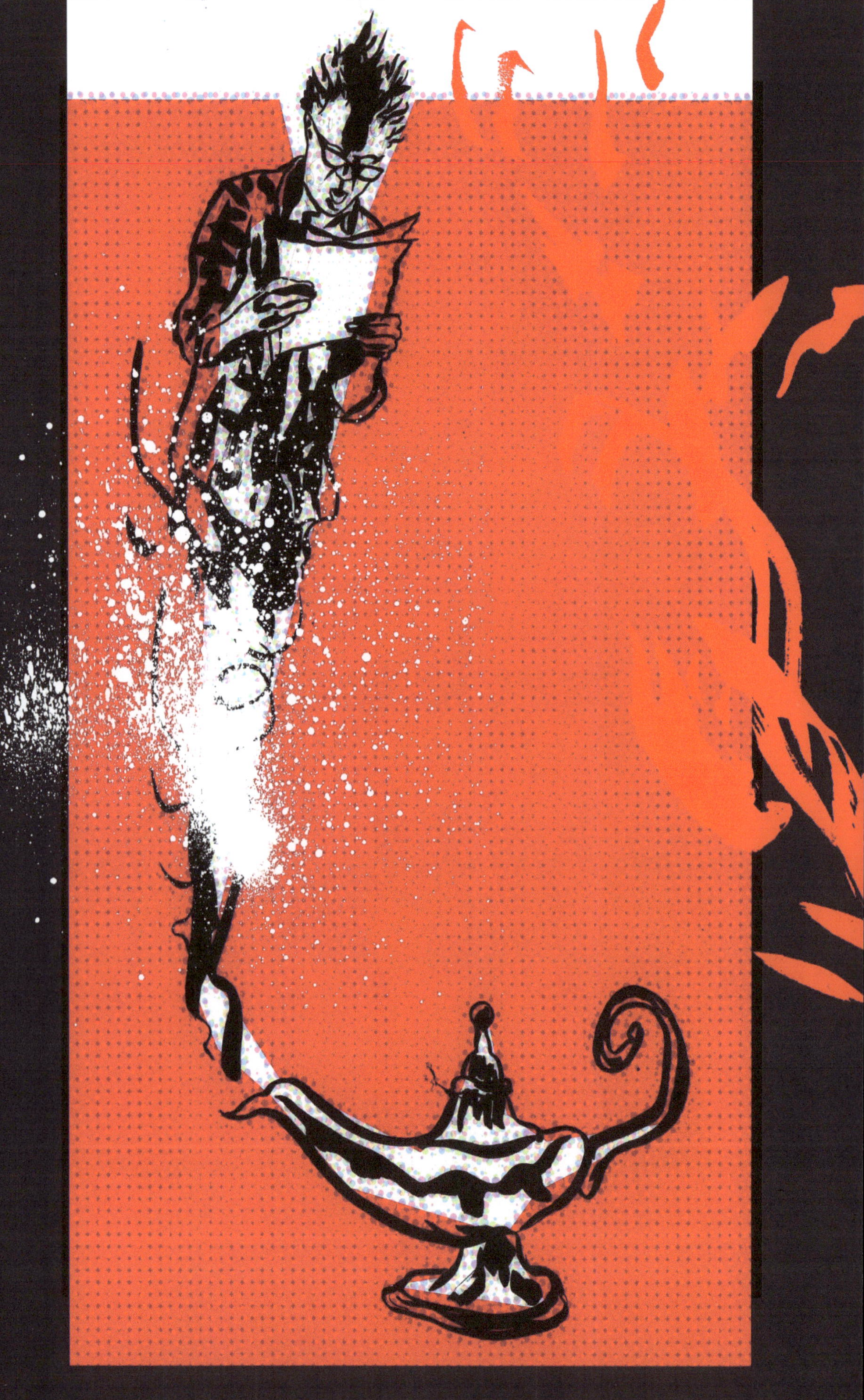

SKINNY DIPPING IN WHITE LAKE

Because there is nothing better
than skinny dipping in White Lake,
I am always taking off my clothes
and diving head first

into a snowball, or on clear blue days
into a cloud or a fake rabbit fur coat,
which gets hot fast, so I have to
take it off, and then I'm naked

again. I am naked and happy and skinnier
than I might be, so I dip myself
in white chocolate. I dip myself
in ivory, in chipped ice, in latex

house paint. The point is to remember
all the times when one feels joy
in one's heart, no matter the occasion
or the clothes one is wearing--or not.

I think I prefer not. I prefer not to.
I walk into the light with a smile
on my face. The white water breaks
against me, and it feels like a polar bear

sleeping with a glacier, the whitest noise
you've ever heard, every frequency
at onee at full volume, jet engine exhaust
and those white white flowers that spasm.

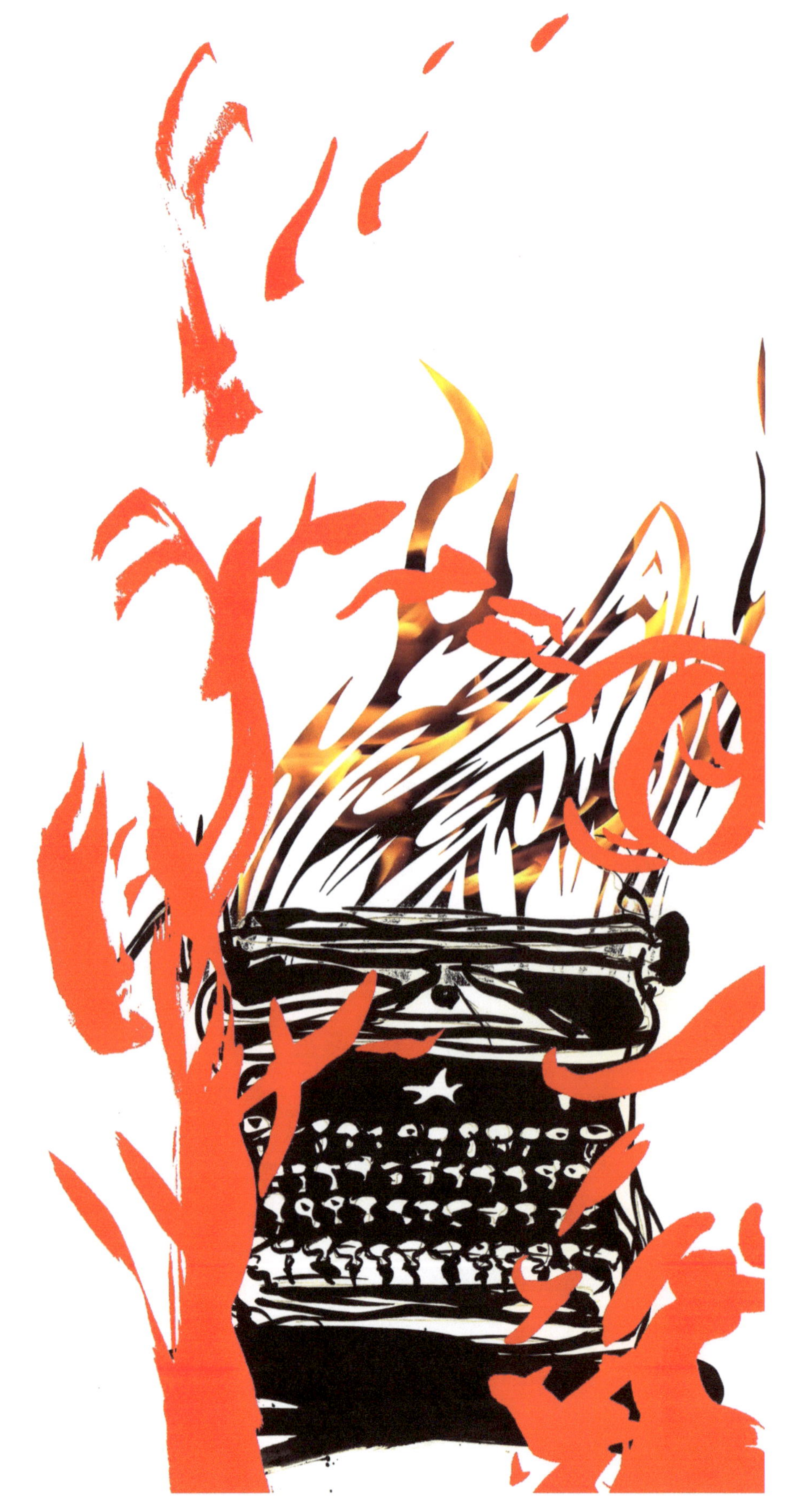

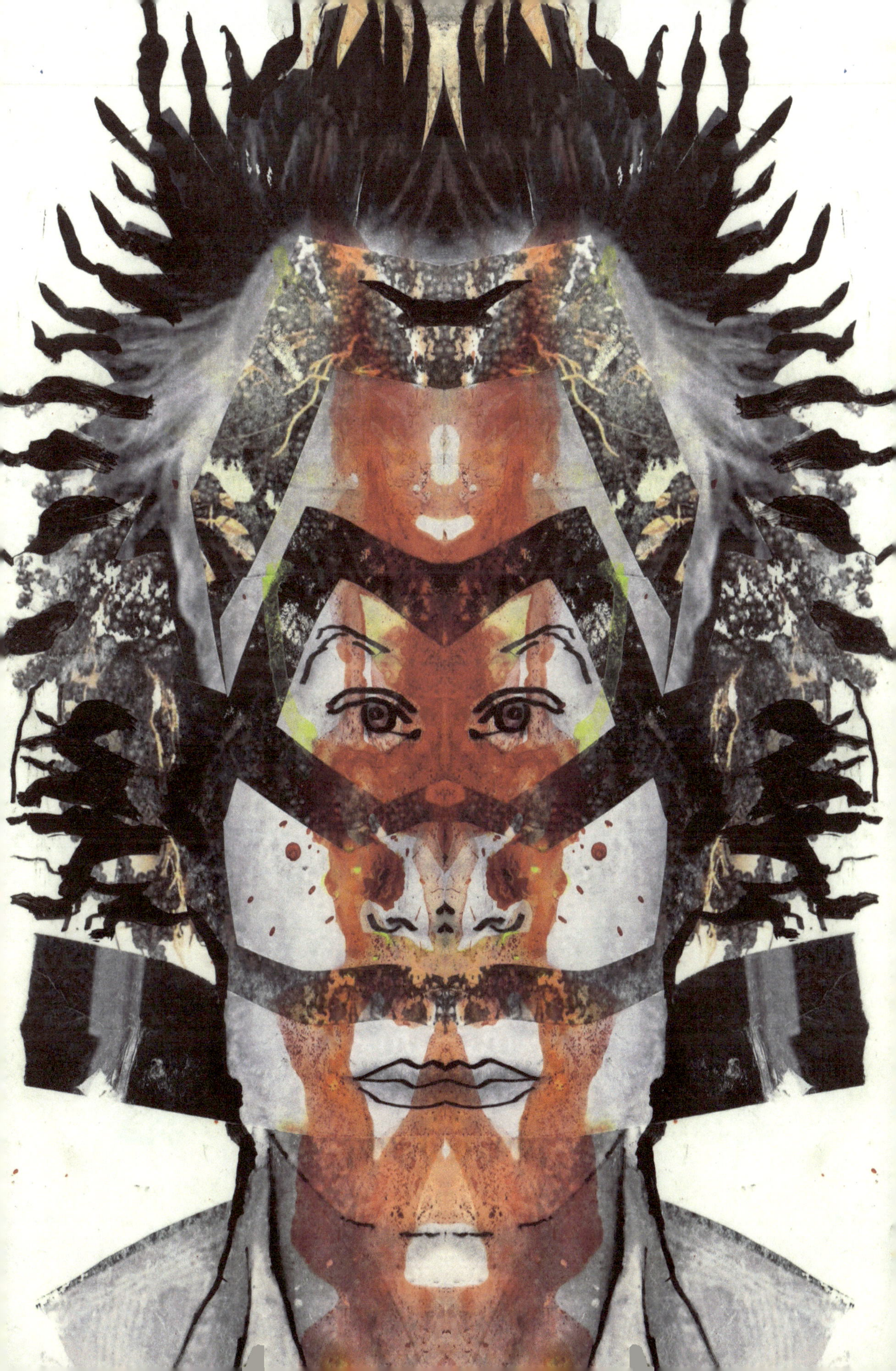

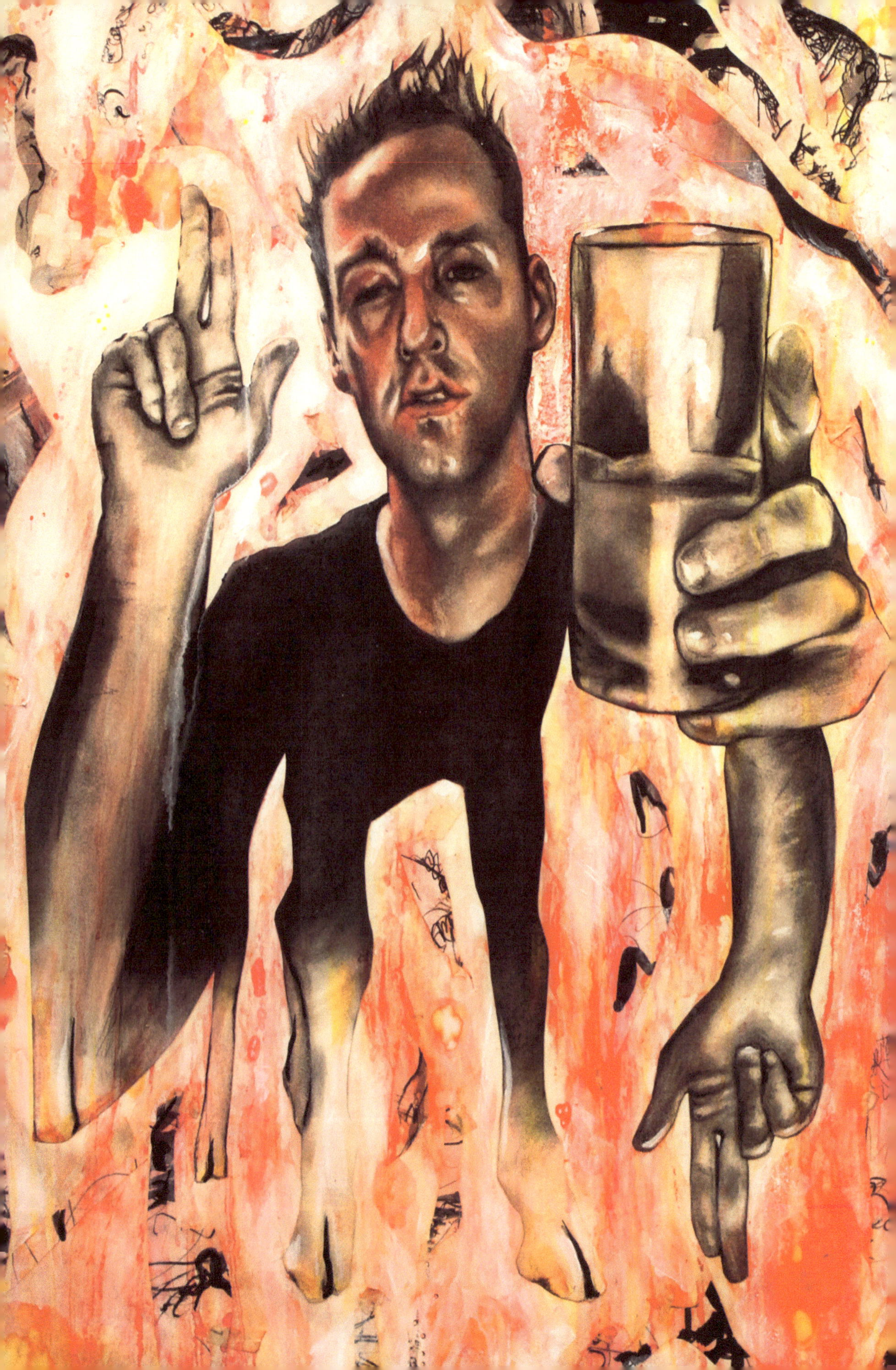

THREE POETS, THREE PAINTERS, TWO DESPOTS, ONE ANGEL

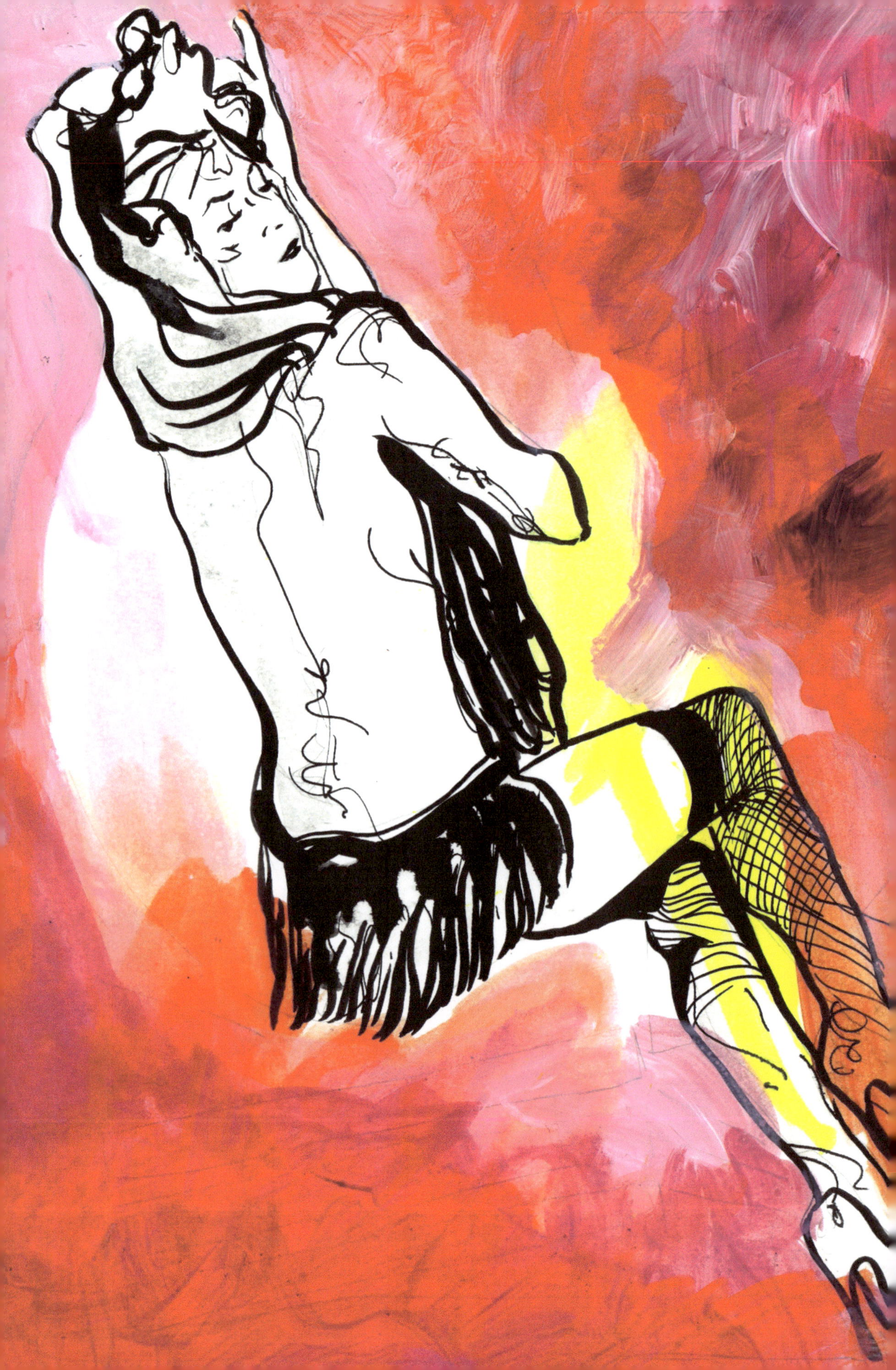

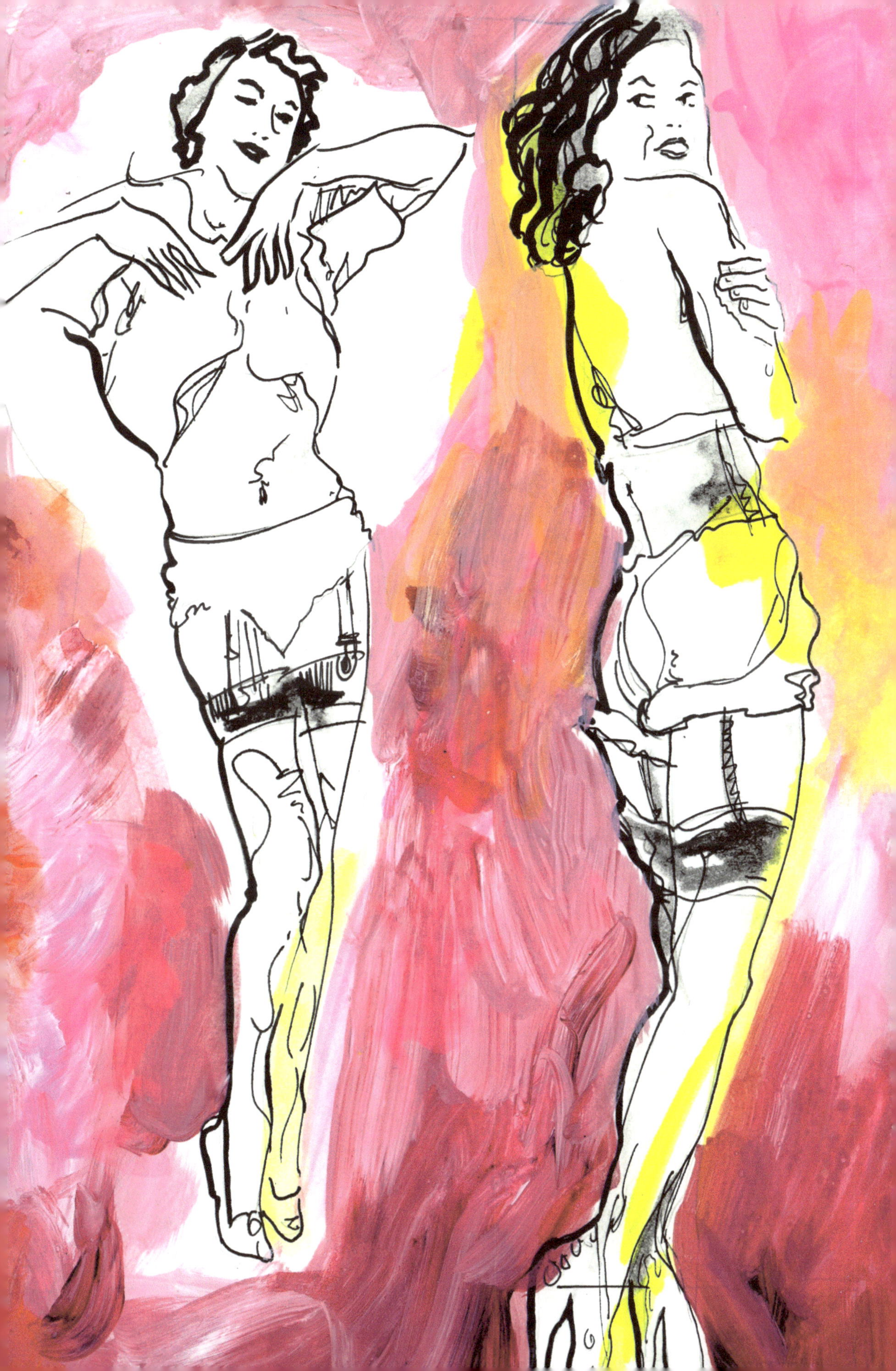

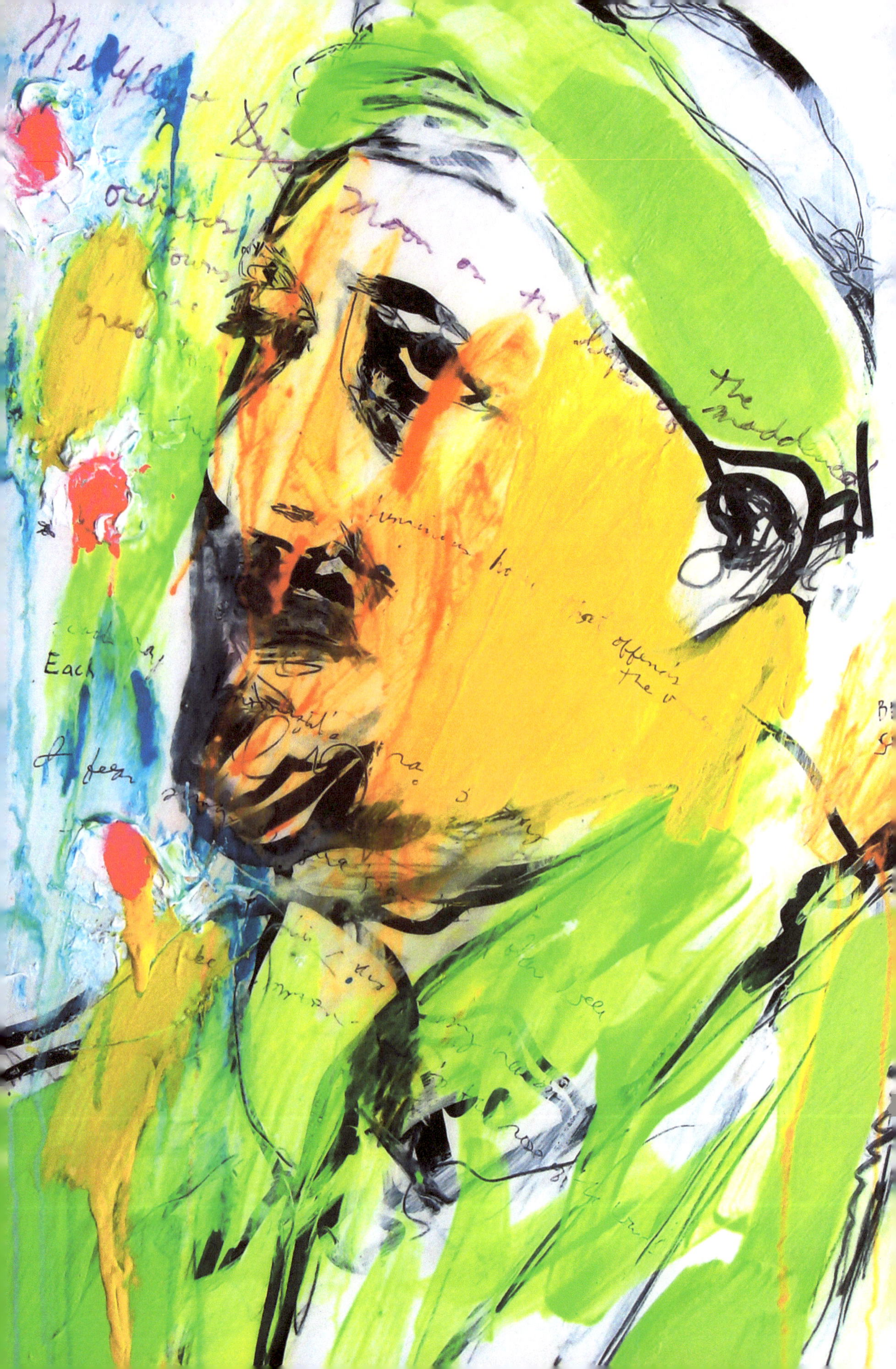

Each

GUILLAUME APOLLINAIRE

My heart will burn up
if I say it will   Skies
are skunks   Skunks are
high   My wife goes to Paris
on a thousand vacations,
and I am none the wiser
I am not even present
when the pictures
become sugar   I read
today's front page, its throbbing
headline, and it stinks
like the future   I cut it out
and paste it on a plaything's doll
I form the word for love
at the neck of your blouse,
and all around this warehouse,
machine guns blur
with my best friend's mouth
O mouth, man is looking
for a new language
no grammarian can legislate
The moon's no trick, it's Icarus
or it's some terrific long line
of sentimental bullshit
I am the bird with only one wing
Who undoes me does me
and who doesn't misses out
The cars driving over the city
don't wait   They go
to the ends of the earth
where they take you

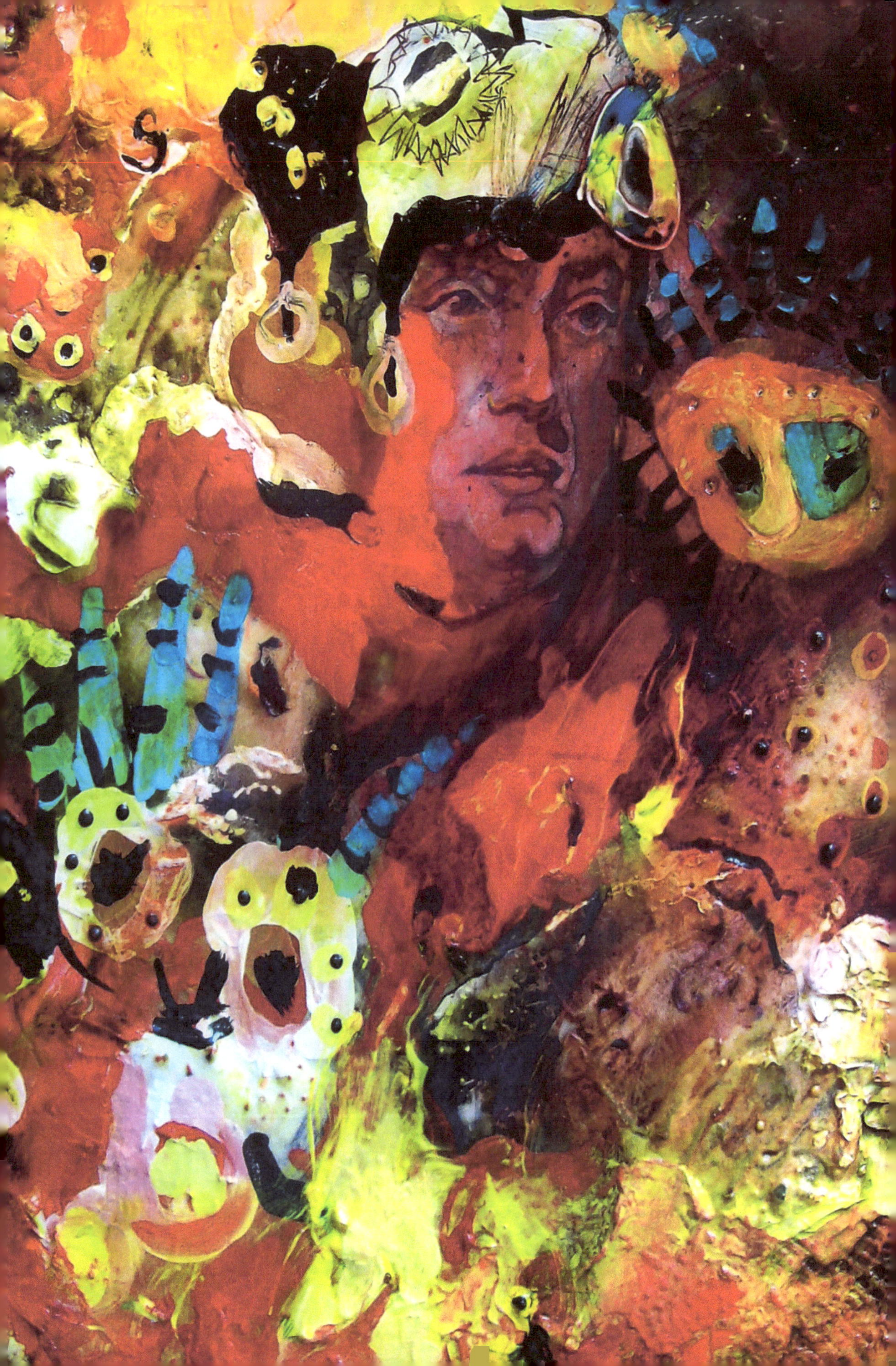

~~SAMUEL TAYLOR COLERIDGE~~

SAMUEL TAYLOR COLERIDGE

My heart will burn up
if I say it will   Amen,
my dear ones   Thy will
be done, etc   Prescribe for me
an anodyne   I've a toothache,
a swollen testicle, a place in my brain
where pigs in the rain sob like a toddler
abandoned by a lake   I'm afraid
to sleep, but also to wake
I nod into the afterlife
and dream about giants
abducting my children,
bears in the kitchen when I wave
my magic wand   Nothing happens
Off again, now at thirty thousand feet,
I nod when the flight attendant
asks me to drink   Sadly, I'll never even know
what a flight attendant is, much less
what one looks like   A damsel
with a dulcimer in a vision once I saw
If I could learn to love
the things I should, instead of those
I shouldn't, I would love you most
of all, my muse of all these many
years   Alas, I am forgotten
and the music in my ears
is that toddler grown older
now screaming just to wake me
Rain splashing down through a hole
in the sun   Follow these sounds
where they take thee

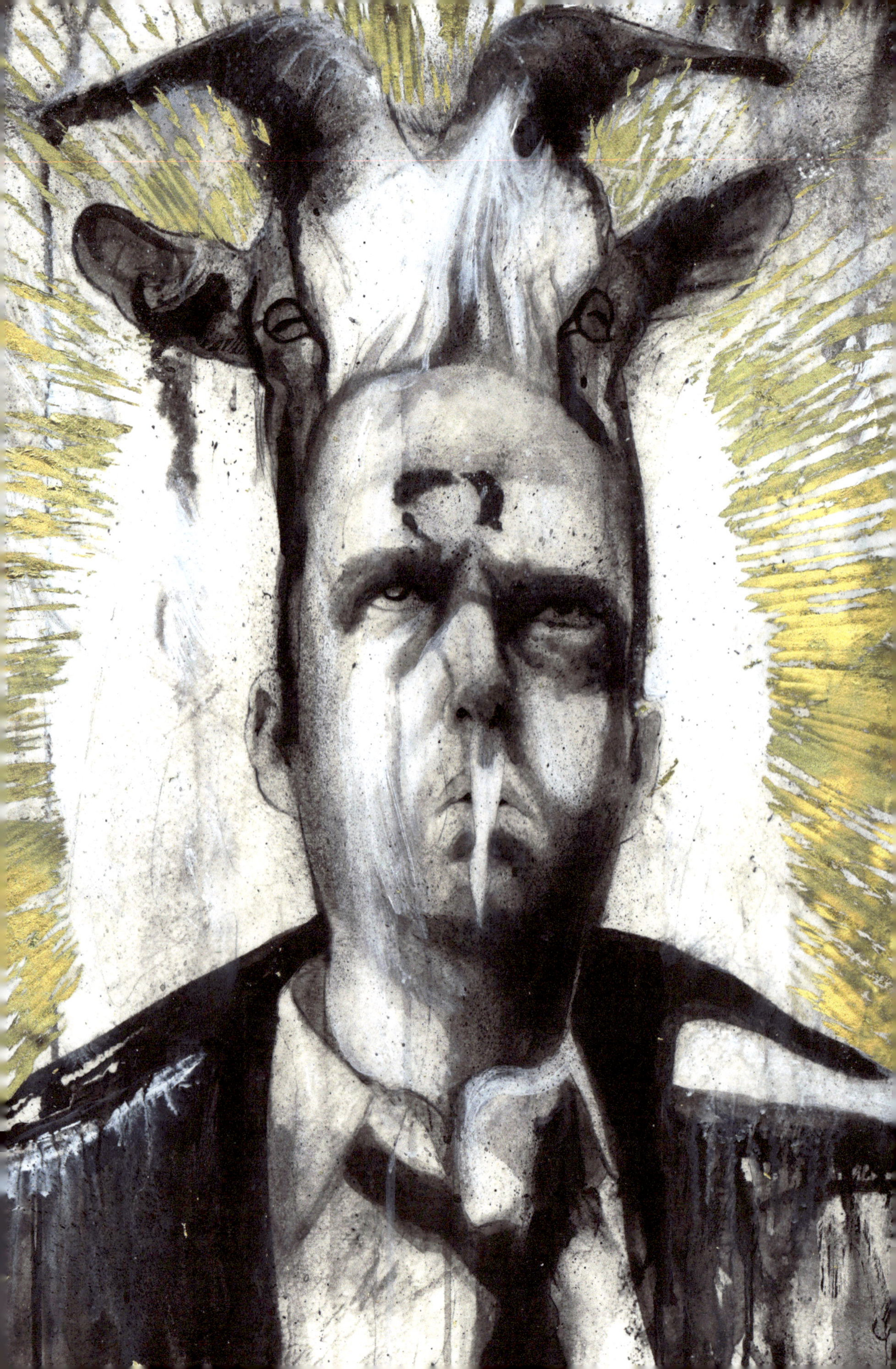

DANTE ALIGHIERI

My heart will burn up
if I say it will   Acheron
Phlegethon Styx   I woke
in a dark wood in the middle
of our life, so that you can do it
too--be lead by the paw
from the microwave to joy
I have no doubt inside
the terrifying dumpster
the citrus-y explosion
of an orange I remember
the forest of suicides,
the boiling blood
and the bone breaking
muck   Some nights, sitting
by myself beneath the stars,
America is unimaginable
out in front of me, its brand
new epic and its fall at the feet
of a truly ancient empire...
Now a dragon roams
my street   Florence
Henderson collapses
in a dream I think
of Beatrice   This life
of movement, one house
to the next   My rhyme scheme
famished, so I weirdly limp along
hoping I can reach you in the future
where they take you

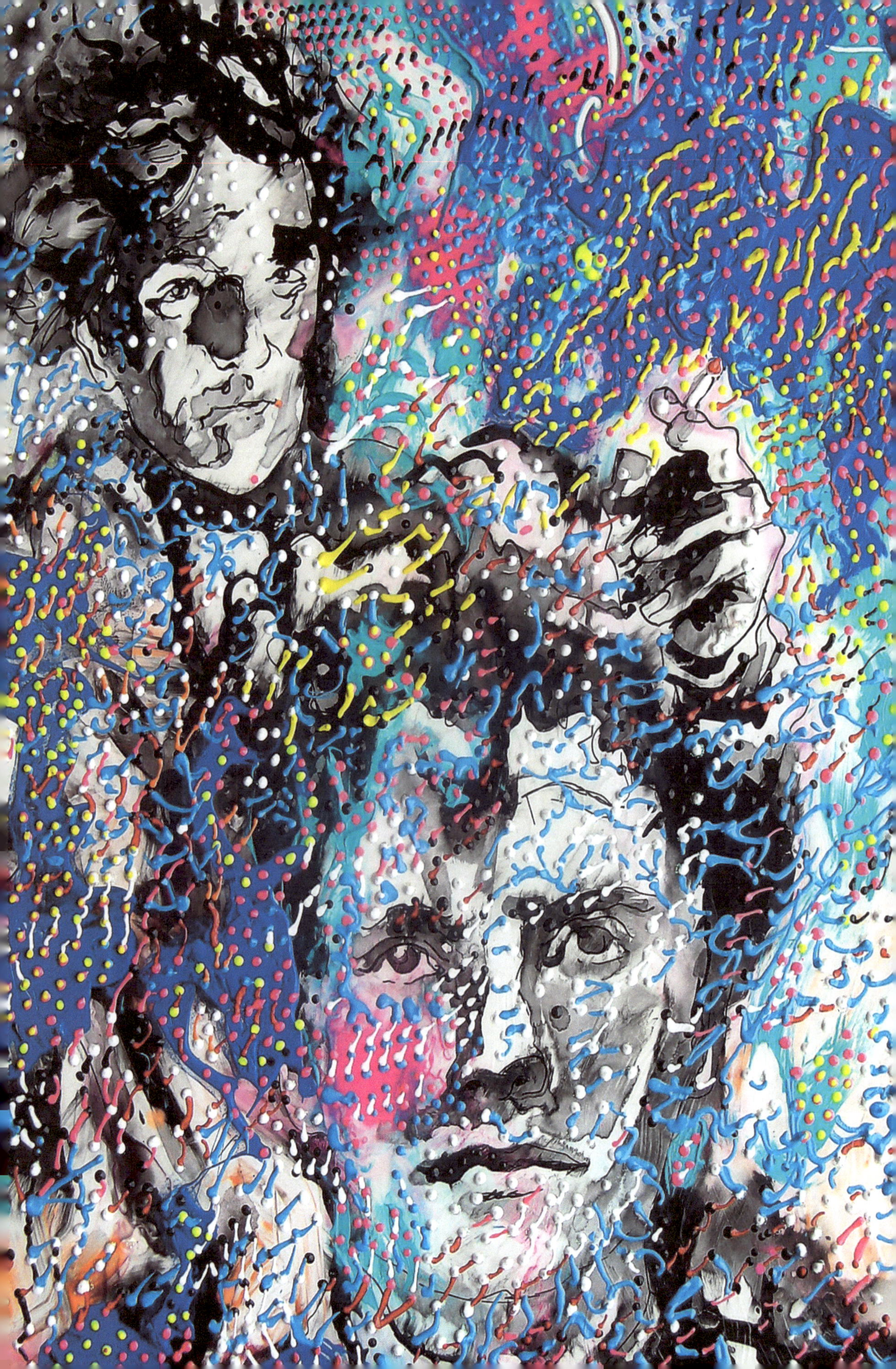

AUSTIN OSMAN SPARE

My heart will burn up
if I say it will   All day long
with a pencil in my hand
Regarding religion, I am
practically zero   The asylums
are crowded, the stage is overrun
I look into the void and the brothel
with my tongue out   Constantly
the asses wag   I think
the young ones are trying
too hard to be the end of me
Cursed be all ye   Corpse devourers
Medicine swallowers   Think ye
Heaven is an infirmary   Only
from negations can I
wholesomely conceive you
I butt a brick wall
with my head sometimes
My alphabet snuggles
in the crotches of witches
Some days my pencil
doesn't move for three months
Of these drawings, I can say only
that prophecy and revelation
are as possible today as they were
in the time of Jonah   Poverty
has made me a ghost at light speed
When my lines suggest a tree
give yourself over
to the leaves
where they take you

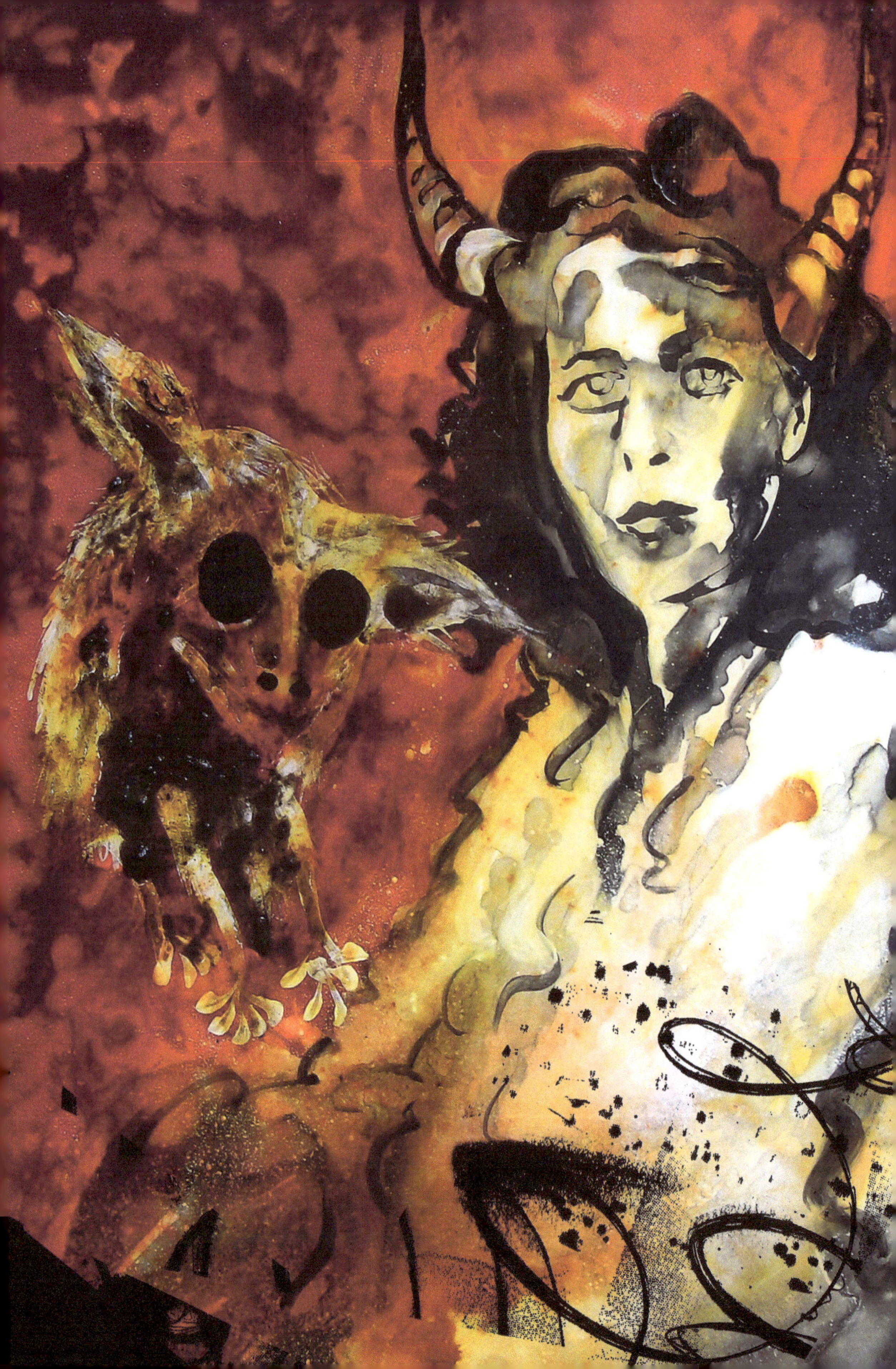

LEONORA CARRINGTON

My heart will burn up
if I say it will   Haven't I
heard this somewhere before
The door to the next room
like a crocodile's intestine
I see through my clothes
I see only stars   You should not
forget the blackest birds in the nest
are only the gods in disguise
to surprise you   Pet them,
pet them warmly   The Ash-
urbanipal Library, the ice cream
shop in Clayton Green
When I tempted Saint Anthony
he died trying to get over me
The gray sky of his face
greener than you'd ever want xexxee
to see   I left him
in the stairwell hurt
I put on my horns and went
fishing with a toaster
No one could guess it,
my secret middle name
Day in and day out
the suits knocked about,
parading by my window
with their *fleurs* hanging out
These images brought to you
by an anxiolytic   Be careful
of the veins in my hands
where they take you

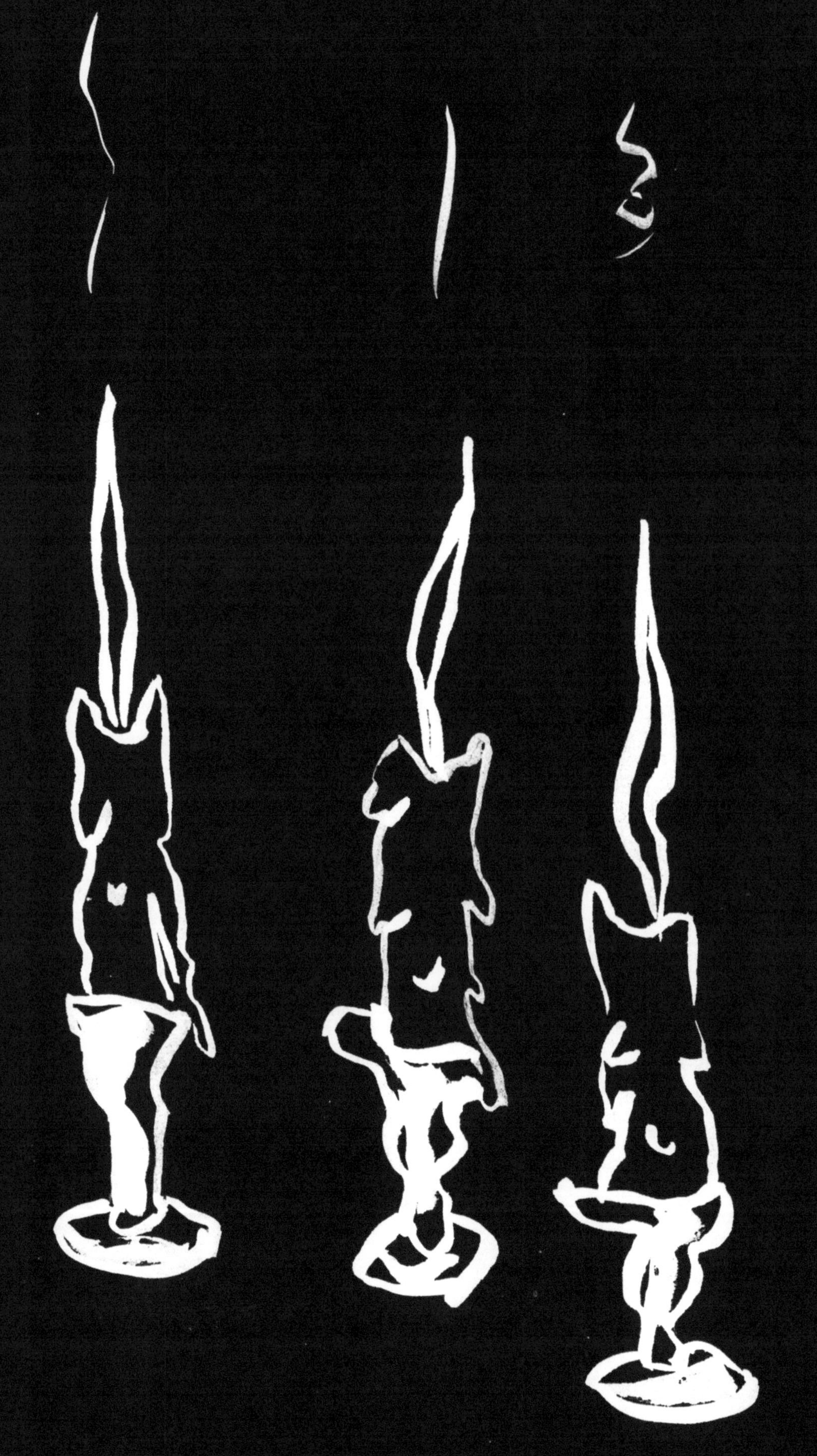

J.M.W. TURNER

My heart will burn up
if I say it will   And yes,
I know the fog won't clear
I have painted my life
in a far away corner, and now
the shadow lingers here
I will be eaten by the sun's sea
monster   My father,
my servant   My closest friends
whisper   My mother, dear deer
in the head lice running over
Everywhere a sparkling
hot ass with its lights out   There is
no way to help myself   The romantic
buffet is large and overflowing
The creature underneath me
as she throws up her hands
I throw up my bathtub
No matter the matter
To hell is forever, or
the soul is sorely debased,
or with flies, the way
others are with child
or the Lady of the Lake
Mine eyes have seen the glory
of my own Dalmatian
I'm a fucking cuckoo clock--
a deluge of yellows
and a figure strapped to it
The pictures don't wander[sic]
where they take you

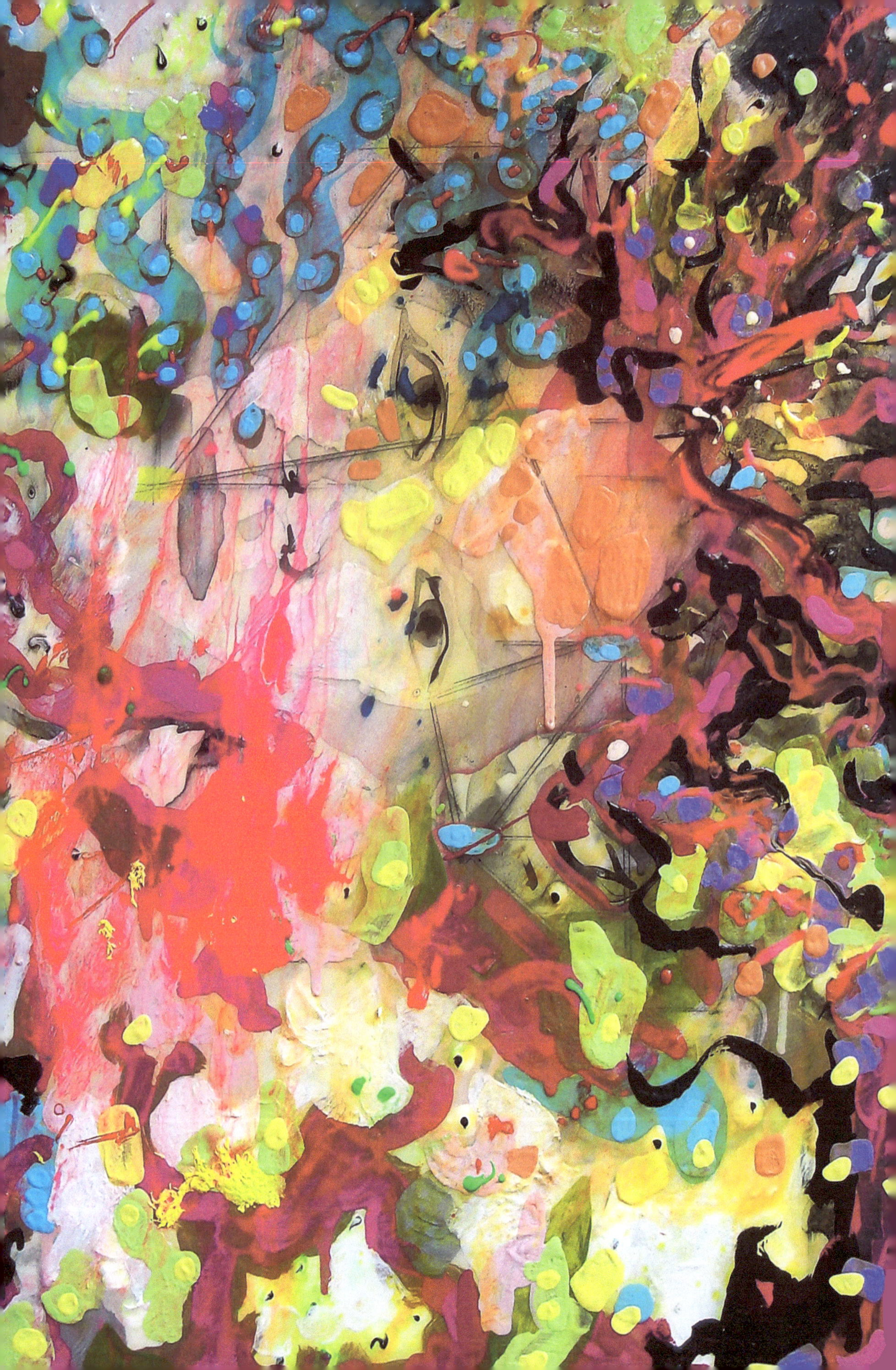

MATT HART

My heart will burn up
if I say it will   And if I say it
will--when I say it will--
you will say trim black shipwreck, or
please sir another crust of bread,
and I will kick in your door
I will blow down your head,
because to me you're a book
that I've already read, but not
a good one   Maybe you will
live forever after in a shoebox,
or maybe I will drown
in the art of what I've done
I write through us now in the basement
I go the whole distance with the frogs
and the lice, football fields
of screamo and the teenager's tights
How weird is that
This is not my finest moment
I am Polyphemus
I am Speaker John Boehner
JonBenet Ramsey
Un-Pledge of Allegiance
I am the eyes soaring
over you, into you,
your nested secret places
Mention this poem
to whomever you confess to
Mercy will come or a shadow
get even   The grass doesn't grow
where I take you

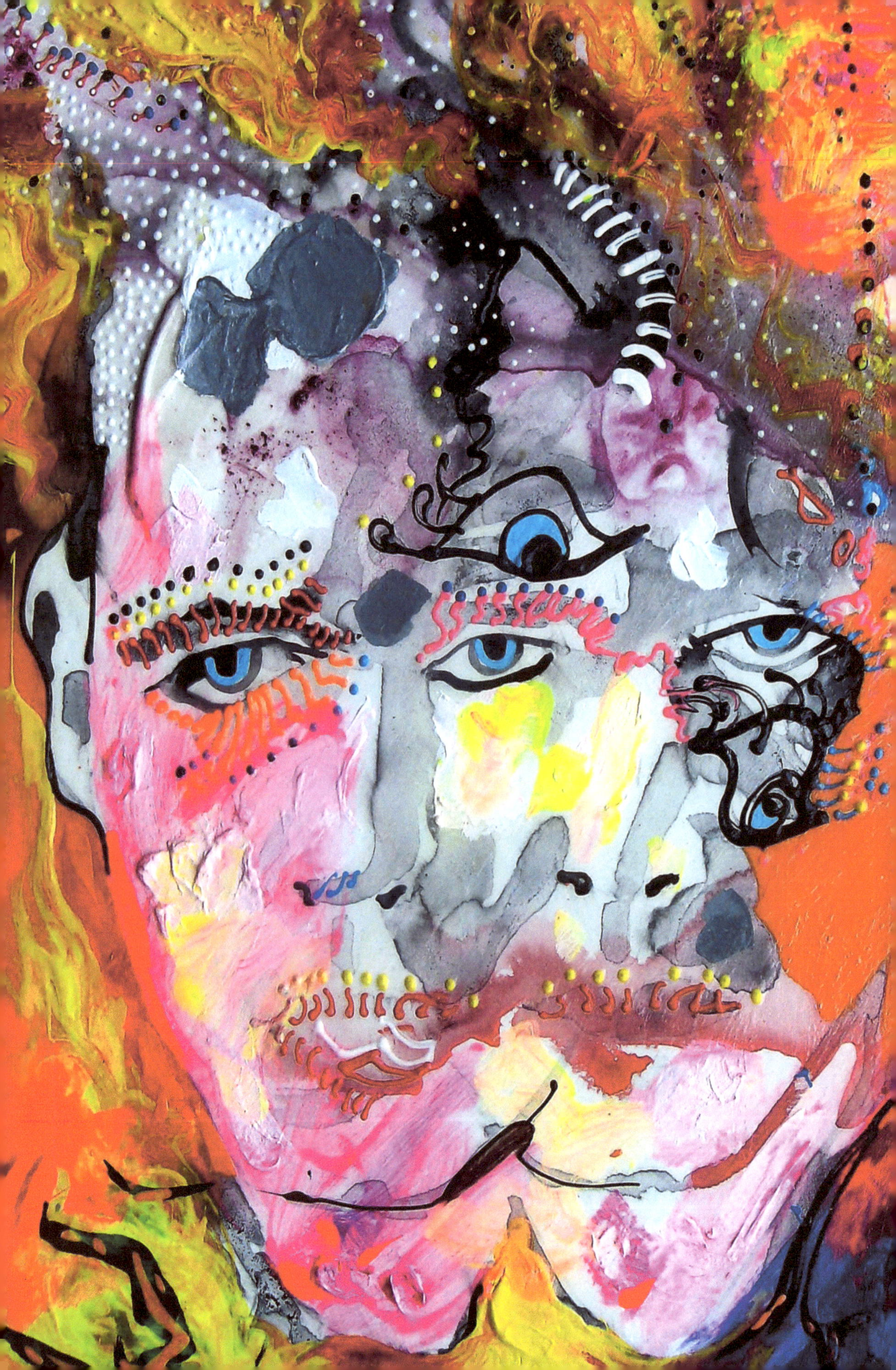

KEN HENSON

My heart will burn up
if I say it will, but it won't
because I would never say that
I would say activated werewolves
and let's just the two of us
drink this High Gravity and think
about how to make the old days
into tomorrow for the next day
And another thing
Do I conjure demons
in the faculty lounge   Yes
Do I imagine automatically
and go where the river
of electricity takes me
Yes   Do I meditate in the nude
in front of the big window
that faces my neighbor's house
No, I do not, but you were hoping
I would say yes, because to you
that would prove something
you've been thinking secretly
about me for a very long time
that I am not who I appear to be,
which is correct   I am the worm
making tunnels in your mind
There is nothing in that apple
that escapes me, and when I kill
this next can,I will open another
and another and another
and that's when you'll see
where they take you

ANNA MENEFEE

My heart will burn up
if I say it will   I have been
missing out of terrible time
The Dante we ploughed through
last spring was amazing,
the recklessness reckless,
the whole town forgiving
The blur of it always blurry,
but sometimes that only makes
the images more revealing
Scylla and Charybdis churning ever
in the sky, Polyphemus wailing
his Odysseus eye   I don't feel like
ruining anything today
This blue light of winter
This quietude that sends me
hanging out among the branches,
which bark themselves in silence
like sprawled dogs to pieces,
awaiting with patience
their spring-loaded greenness xx
to spring, to blast^site   It's clear
I don't know what to say
I don't know why the books
don't work, how the buds
can fail to notice
and put us on notice
even harder than ever before
in this life   What has always worked
for me is a face full of stars,
connecting the dots
where they take you

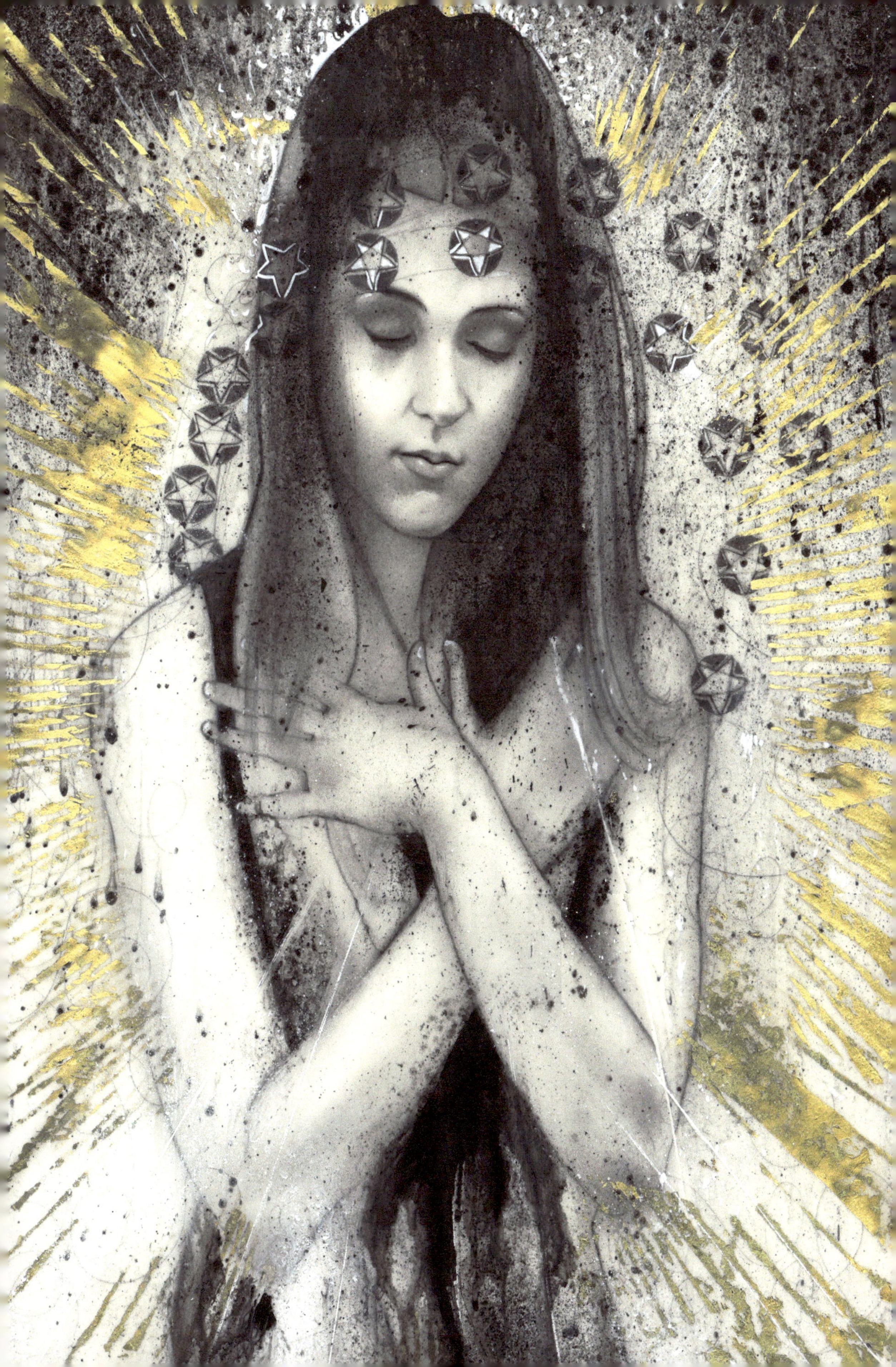

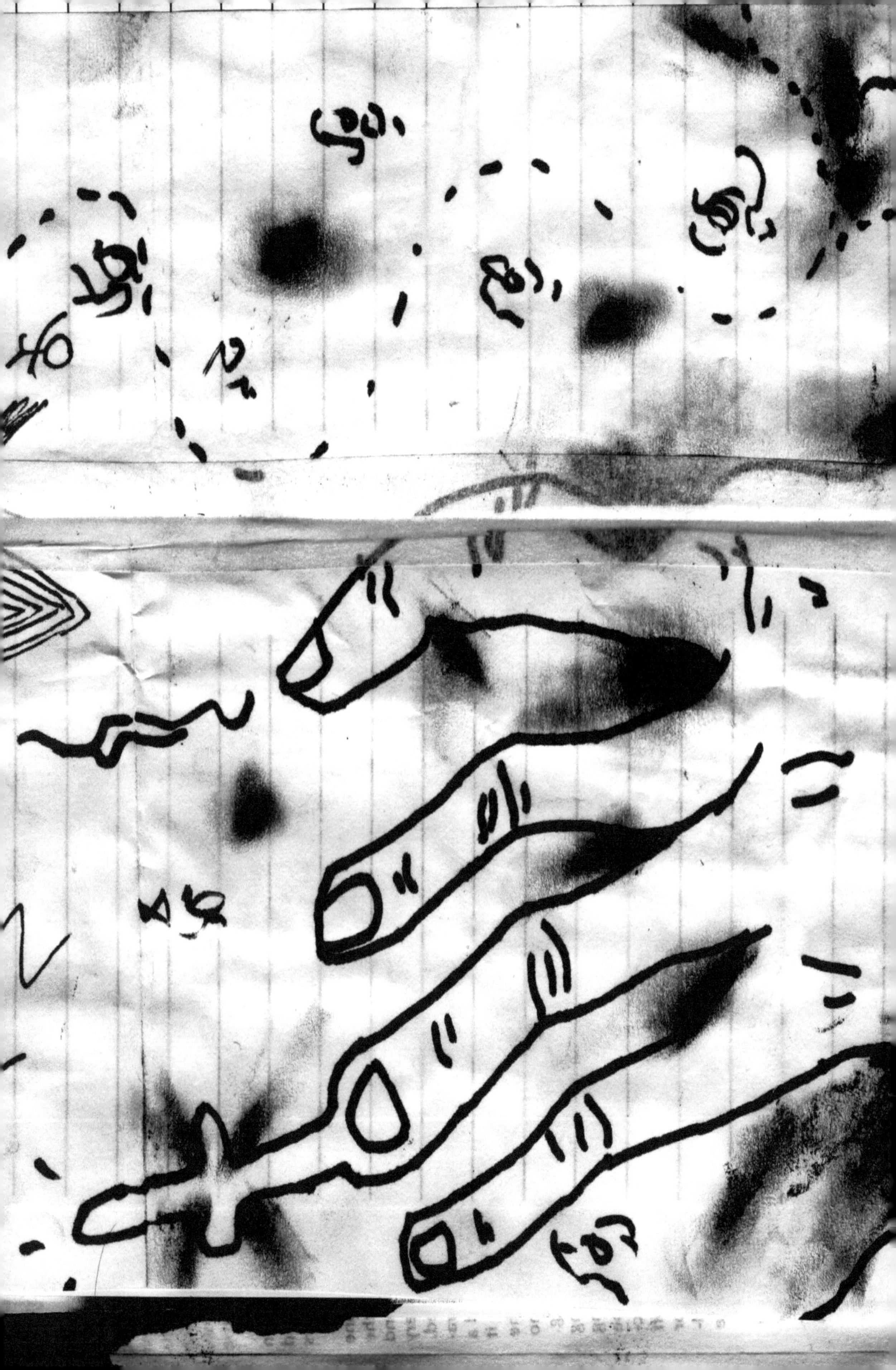

THE POWER IS WRONG

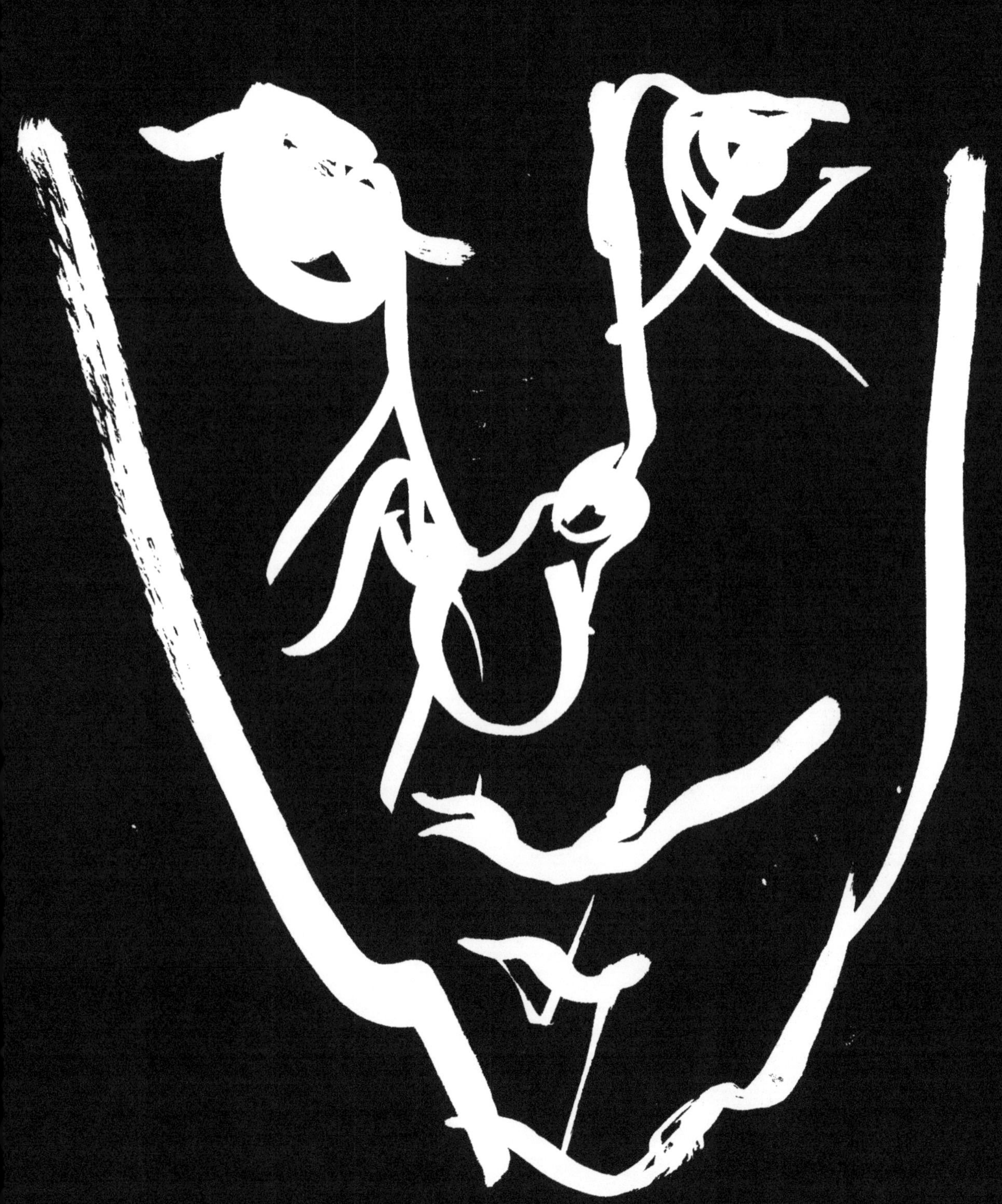

PAINTER OF LIGHT

Lately, I'm faking more than usual
Often in the night when I fall
behind a dumpster   My hair is too long, but not
unusually impossible   It's weird to have been once
so incredibly with clouds   You might know me
around the fire telling stories   When I collapse
roasting meat, put a fork in a potato
I used to paint the apple trees, but got tired
of all the horses and farmhands laying on me,
tired of the light sneaking into the wound,
making everything soft with its pinkish
corrections   The goal is to become less,
not more, human being   Someday
when I blast into a subway station...
You black out, and that's it   The moment's
forgotten already before it happens   Of course,
you never really existed in the first place
Every decision you ever made xgxinxx against
your nature   Every fucking vote
you ever cast against your interests
When I fall behind a butcher's block or down
the basement stairs, my only wish is
trembling things   Don't imagine them
lightly   The birds or the leaves
or the teeth between my teeth   You are
there   Once I built a stadium
and lit it to perfection   I filled it full
of gravity and watched the revolutions,
the executions, watched as the worms struggled
in through all my pockets and out
through the terror of everyone ixxxxxxxdxxxx
in attendance, breaking up the earth
that it continues forever   I am
but a tear in the mouths of those departing
My halogen headlamp, so I never think to sleep
I'm afraid of the dark where I find you
counting blessings, but delighted to see
the gaping hole in your sheep   I will eat
for both of us   The miracle of no One's home
No one's there to back you up   No one
with an ear for when I crash down the mountain
and take your stupid head through a window
to a meadow   Grass staining red delicious apple
while you wait

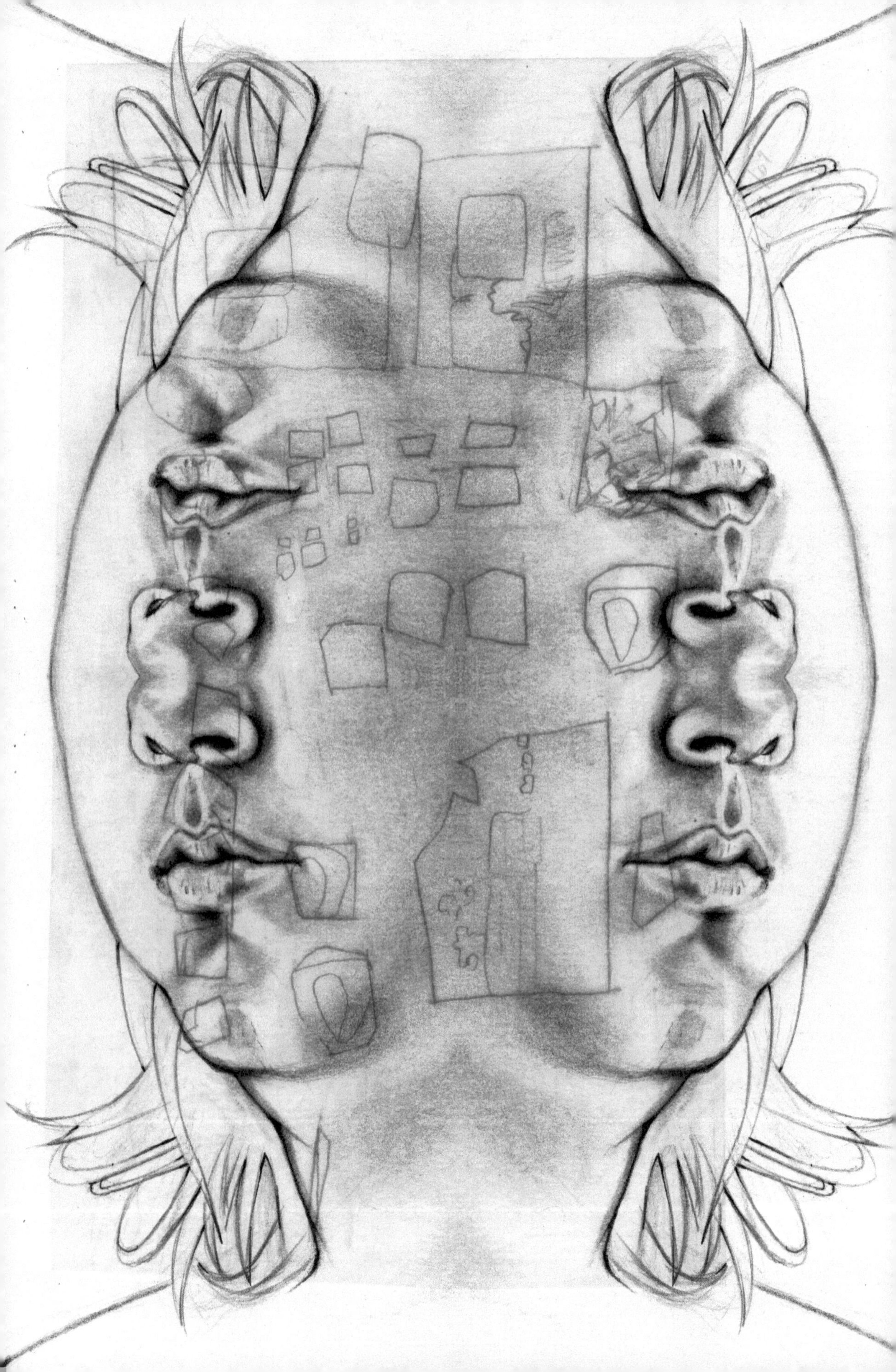

~~LANDSCAPE OF A VOMITING~~
~~LANDSCAPE OF A VOMITING~~

LANDSCAPE OF A VOMITING

Plenitude. And I am on my knees
with little starlings near a red lake house,
welling up with tears, firetrucks,
the steeples of distant churches. This is

Vermont. Lake Eden Mills. Where Lorca
once walked, and now a parade
of us comes rolling in in blood
and breath and afternoon. It's April.

Chill wind, mist, and hangover.
There's still a lot of snow up here.
The lake's a melting blanket, whiteout
of stretching blankness. I feel a thousand times

sicker than ever. If ever. Sorry I'm so fucking
useless, I write later to Amanda, I don't know
how I wound up drinking so much last night,
but I did, and now I can't stop

crying when we stand around reading
"Double Poem of Lake Eden" and "Living
Sky," first Spanish, then English, then English,
then Spanish. The actual sky's alive with its fusion

reactor. I'm trying too hard to really be any good.
I know just enough to be an idiot.

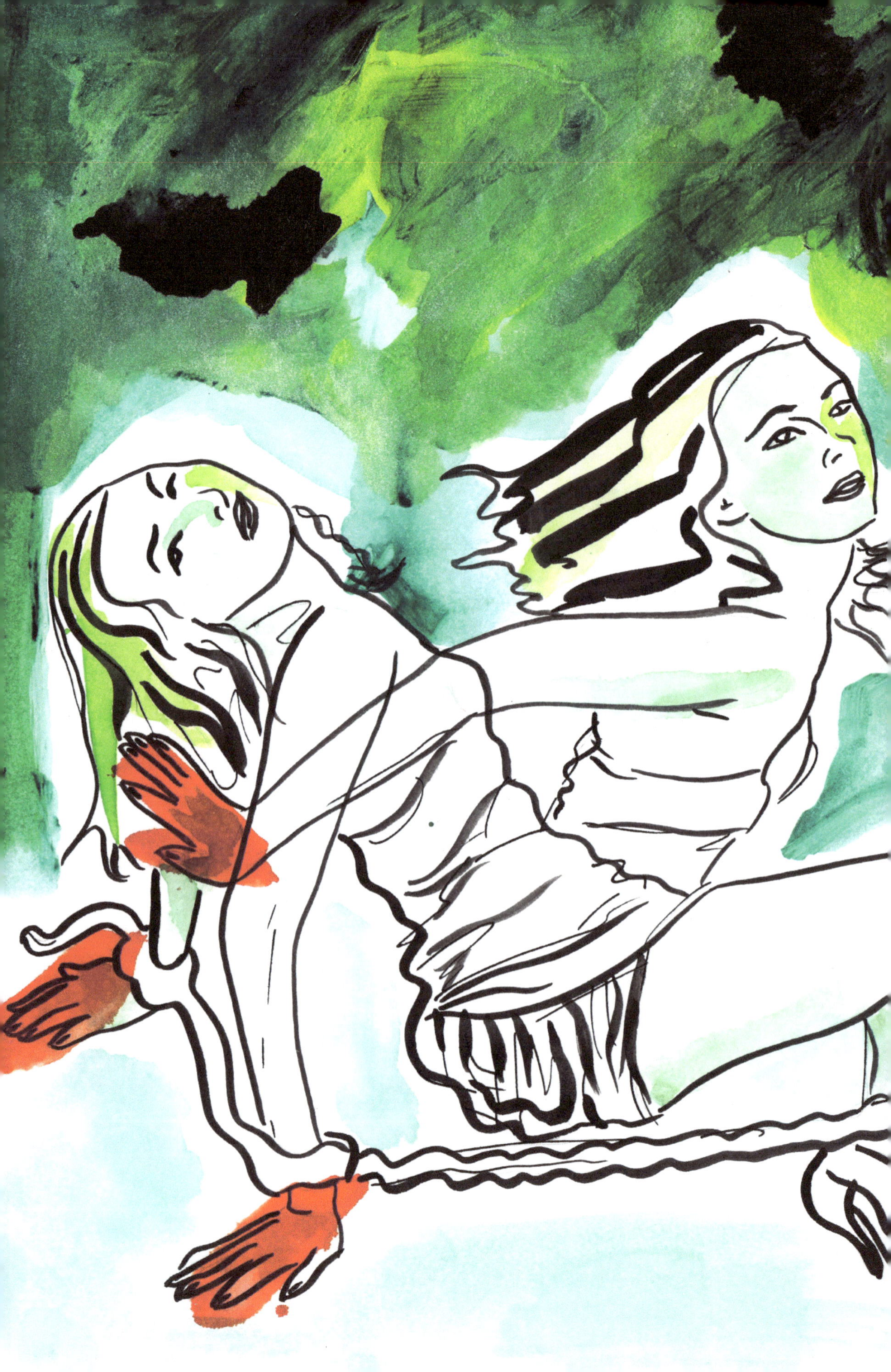

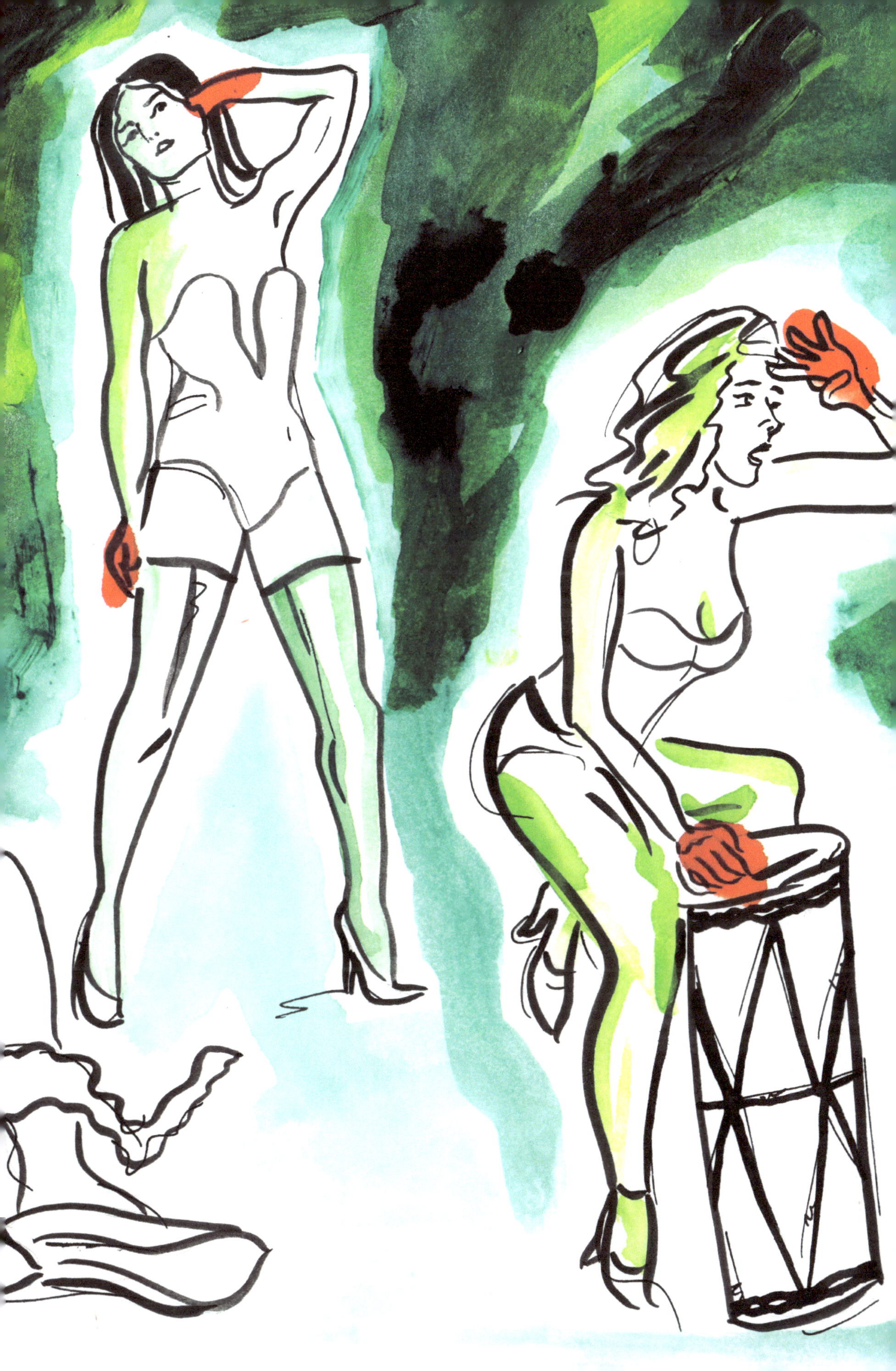

THE POWER IS WRONG

Cherry pits and stems on the edge
of the kitchen sink. I'm already
baffled how this didn't go my way.
I thought I might write the phrase
"cherry red jeep," because you
told me I should, but instead
I've wound up on the threshold
of some imaginary idyll eating cherries
and looking out the window
at my neighbor not watering his tomatoes.
Dot dot dot. And that I've already spent
three weeks in this state says something
about how reluctant I am to brag
about it, but nothing about why
opening my mouth hurts so much.
Maybe it's the roasted Scotch Bonnets
I downed in a shot, eyes welling up
in the heat, because it's hot and I'm not
feeling so hot. I'm feeling loaned out
to buy a boarded-up house and no plan
to make it better. If you want to see
the body, come and find me
in the grass stain. The concrete
circumstances I can never manage to say,
but somehow I manage to say killing
a lot of ripe deer with my teeth, or killing
my best friend for throwing me
in the lake, killing my wife and little girl
because I'm angry. I'm angry about
birds. I'm angry about value. I'm angry
about worm holes and black holes
and drifting off to sleep, and the day-
dreaming dream of never waking up.
Hamlet, Prince of Denmark.
The Whale that swallowed Jonah.
Thales and Heraclitus and Kierkegaard
and Whitehead. Too much and not enough
of everything at once--I wrote that already,
but I don't remember where--maybe
at length the intellectuals will enlighten.
I smile at the thought of their continuing
absence. Oblivion and Jesus. Go
to your monster and never come out.
I eat another cherry, and I swallow the pit.
I swallow the stem. I swallow a swallow

through the window I wallow.
Let us be pigs, black mud coursing
through us. Let us take the light
from delight and make it obvious.
I want to swing from murder
to rapture in an instant. Take off
your clothes, delicious young people.
Take off your clothes,
follow me.

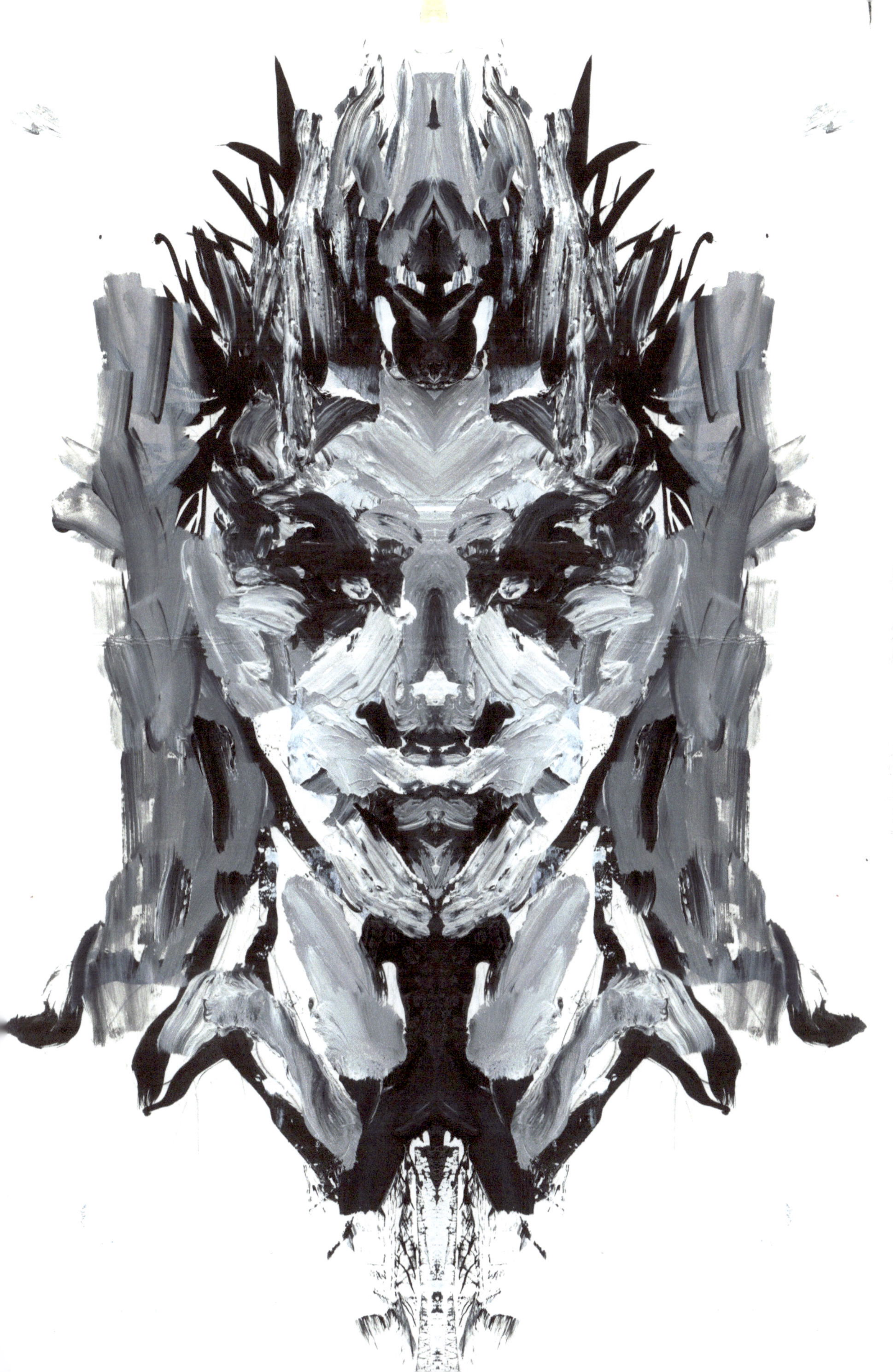

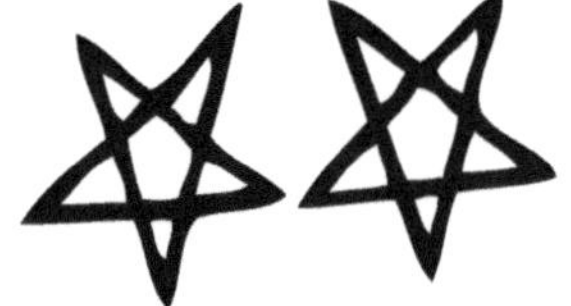

BLUE JAY SLAYER
Notes/Acknowledgments

Ken and Matt would like to thank the following friends, accomplices, and loved ones for their help, support, and enthusiasm regarding this project: Paula Menetrey and Isabelle Henson, Melanie and Agnes Hart, Chuck Byrd and Betsy Young, Mary Anne and Mike Cowgill, and Eric Appleby and Tricia Suit.

Additionally, special thanks go to: Alice Bag, Gary Jackson & Dave Lombardo xrxthexblurbx (for the blurbs!), blue jays (because they're birds), and, of course, Slayer (because they're SLAYER).

Massive thanks also to the editors of the following journals where some of these poems first appeared, often in different form and/or with different titles: *The American Reader*, *Barn Owl Review*, *Cerise Press*, *The Fiddleback*, *Ghost Town*, xx and *Hidden City Quarterly*.

"Skinny Dipping in White Lake" was written in response to the prompt "Skinny dipping in White Lake" for Poems While You Wait, Dose Market, Chicago, Sunday Dec. 15th, 2013. The poem originally appeared on the Poems While You Wait Tumblr page Jan. 23, 2014. Thanks Kathleen Rooney and Eric Plattner for including me.

"The TV Is on the TV Is on the TV" is for Chloë Bell.

"Golden" is for Billy Golden.

The painting "Etidorhpa" is property of The Lloyd Library and Museum.

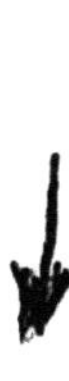

www.ingramcontent.com/pod-product-compliance
Lightning Source LLC
LaVergne TN
LVHW070138110826
845147LV00002B/280

* 9 7 8 0 6 9 2 3 2 5 8 5 8 *